NATIVES PREFERRED

By

CAROLINE DORMON

with Illustrations by the Author

Native trees and flowers for every location.

Baton Rouge
CLAITOR'S BOOK STORE
1965

Published and for sale by:

CLAITOR'S BOOK STORE

241 North Street, P. O. Box 239

BATON ROUGE, LOUISIANA 70821

For

Elizabeth Lawrence

ACKNOWLEDGMENTS

For answering my many questions I wish to express my appreciation to the following:

Dr. Edgar Anderson, Missouri Botanical Garden, St. Louis, Mo.

B. Y. Morrison, Pass Christian, Mississippi.

Harold Epstein, Larchmont, New York.

Elizabeth Lawrence, Charlotte, North Carolina.

Carl Starker, Jennings Lodge, Oregon.

Claude Barr, Prairie Gem Ranch, Smithwick, South Dakota.

Lester Roundtree, Carmel, California.

Mary G. Henry, Gladwyne, Pennsylvania.

William L. Hunt, Chapel Hill, North Carolina.

Dorothy E. Hansell, New Providence, New Jersey.

Willie May Kell, Wichita Falls, Texas.

Margaret Scruggs Carruth, Dallas, Texas.

Mrs. H. R. Totten, Chapel Hill, North Carolina.

John Lambert, Wixom, Mich.

Harry E. Elkins, Grosse Pointe, Mich.

Dr. Clair Brown, Botany Dept., Louisiana State University, Baton Rouge.

Mrs. Harry Meek, Little Rock, Arkansas.

Emily S. Parcher, for permission to quote from her book, Shady Gardens.

I wish to express deep appreciation for the writings and letters of the late W. W. Ashe.

TABLE OF CONTENTS

Rock Gardens Go Native 3

Bulbs Are Easy 20

The Shady Trail 33

Wild and Sunny 44

Flowering Trees and Shrubs 55

Evergreens 95

Vines 107

Ground-Covers 117

By All Means Have Pond 127

The Glory of Autumn 137

Winter 157

Grow Wild Flowers from Seed 165

The Wild Iris 175

Set The Table for The Birds 182

Roadsides 191

Garden Pictures 199

Bibliography 205

Index 207

WHY?

THE question may be asked, why use native plants? The logical answer to this is, why not? If a tree or flower is beautiful, easy to grow, and fits into the landscape, it is the best plant for that location. First, and most important, such species are adaptable to local conditions. Second, by using native plants, gardens and public grounds can display the typical beauty of each region. The well-known landscaper, Jens Jensen* repeatedly emphasizes the value and importance of using trees and flowers indigenous to each area, rather than bringing in species from afar.

This book is not written for those who still cling to the Old World style of formal gardening, with stiff clipped hedges and beds of flowers in geometrical designs. It is for those who love the informality of Nature, with softly rounded masses of foliage, and flowers scattered freely by her hand. To see perfect landscaping, go to the edge of a woodland, observe tall trees for background, see how these step down to massed Dogwood, Hawthorn, and Wild Plum, with a flowery meadow or old field filling the forespace.

It is not strange that our first settlers turned to their mother countries for plants. Yet when reading Bartram's Travels**, with his lyrical descriptions of shrubs and trees he encountered, one wonders that any gardener could have desired more than these. There were the famous *Franklinia* and *Gordonia lasianthus*, both related to the Camellia; *Azaleas* in colors never seen before;

---

* Siftings and The Clearing, by Jens Jensen.
** The Travels of William Bartram.

vii

Kalmia and *Rhododendron*; great blazing *Hibiscus*; several *Magnolias*; and dozens of other species. He collected these, grew them in his garden at Philadelphia, and it would seem that this would have inspired others to follow his example. But at that time travel was very limited and it is probable that few saw his garden. In contrast, seeds and plants he sent to England were enthusiastically received, and some of the loveliest *Azaleas* and *Rhododendrons* in that country are hybrids of our beautiful American species. Later, other collectors sent our native plants across the sea, and some of these came home to make their debuts in America. Among them are *Tradescantia* (named for the King's Gardener), and *Phlox drummondii*.

I am often amazed by gardeners who ask, "What is that beautiful thing?" On being told it is an American plant they exclaim, "You don't mean this is *wild*?" It is true that sometimes flowering shrubs are so crowded in the woods they do not display their charms to best advantage. When cut back, carefully moved, and planted where they can assume their natural forms, they respond gratefully.

But a word of warning: if this book should cause gardeners to rush out, dig indiscriminately, and bring in plants from the woods, I shall wish I had not spoken. Some years ago I took Dr. Edgar Wherry (University of Pennsylvania) to get pictures of an unusual form of *Phlox divaricata* near Shreveport, Louisiana. When we reached the spot, we had to move a brush-heap to find *one* clump to photograph. "Why," I exclaimed, "They used to cascade all down that bluff!" "What became of them?" he asked. I shrugged, "Diggin' Women." When asked for an explanation I gave it. When he said he would like to write that up for Wild Flower, of which he was Editor, I agreed—on condition he would not mention my name. Some of my best friends are "Diggin' Women"! It happened I knew who had left this lovely spot denuded of its lavender carpet.

And now we have Diggin' *Men*. So many are becoming interested in gardening, and when a man sees a native plant he admires he must have it, and distance does not deter him. Of course anyone who truly loves wild flowers will learn to study the natural conditions before moving a plant, and if unable to reproduce these, will leave it in Nature's care. When the road-making machines are coming soon, one can take up rare plants and reset them in a suitable site, not necessarily a garden.

Unless one is so fortunate as to own a place with small streams, or springs and bogs, Pitcher-plants, Orchids, Swamp Candles (*Orontium*), and others should not be attempted. More and more, private owners of suitable areas are preserving rare native species. For many years Mary G. Henry has collected and grown wild flowers at Gladwyne, Pennsylvania, and has saved some unusual plants from being exterminated. She has also introduced a number to horticulture. In North Carolina, William L. Hunt has collected and grown many beautiful plants in a natural woodland which he owns. Both of these flower lovers have established foundations, so their valuable collections will never be lost. In South Mississippi, B. Y. Morrison and Frank and Sara Gladney are preserving species native to the region, and adding others. The Gladneys have formed the John James Audubon Foundation.

The National Parks all have areas set apart where wild flowers are rigidly protected, with only trails winding through. Most state parks, too, are trying to save the native species. Chicot State Park, Louisiana, has recently established an arboretum where southern trees and shrubs are being planted. The famous Arnold Arboretum has extensive plantings of species indigenous to the United States. The wild gardens at the Brooklyn Botanic, New York Botanical Garden, and the Missouri Botanical Gardens are famous for their beauty and interest. In the Mid-west, Jens Jensen landscaped a number of parks possessing distinctive charm, for he used native trees and shrubs almost exclusively.

Some large private estates are giving more and more attention to American plants. Hodges Gardens (Many, Louisiana) includes four thousand acres under fence, where fires and grazing animals are kept out. Only a small part of this property is occupied by planned gardens, while over the hills and between sandstone ledges Nature's own plantings are coming back. Callaway Gardens (Pine Mountain, Georgia) has winding drives, displaying thousands of native Azaleas, Mountain Laurels, and other local species in breath-taking beauty.

Australia has set aside thousands of acres as preserves to save her wonderful flora. Every state in our land should own an area devoted to the preservation of trees and flowers of each region. One of the most overwhelming attractions of the popular Smoky Mountains National Park is the beautiful display of blossoming Rhododendrons in spring, and the amazing coloring of Maples and Sourwood in fall.

There are many factors which contribute to the disappearance of our wild flowers, such as grazing animals, and crowding out by undesirable trees and vines. But the most destructive animal on earth is man. The careless manner in which forests are cut for lumber and pulpwood, with consequent fires, has depleted the groves of Dogwood, Azalea, Fringe Tree, and other lovely species. The "exploding population" is pushing additions ever farther from cities, covering natural gardens. More and more, wide highways are being created, with the terrible bulldozer taking out great swathes of flowery bogs and woodlands. We should save as much as possible before it is too late. Wouldn't it be a splendid thing if all the garden clubs in America would take part of the time spent in flower arranging and put it into creating wild flower gardens?

When possible to find native plants listed, it is much wiser to purchase them from a reliable nursery, where they should have good root systems and be adapted to cultivation. Plant dealers who simply go out and collect on order should be avoided, for they are denuding our country-side of its natural beauty. Sad to say, some of our Market Bulletins are guilty on this count. Tingle Nursery Company deserves a citation, for the owners are propagating rare native shrubs from layers, cuttings, and seeds. This takes time, and many nurserymen are too impatient to avail themselves of these methods.

Of course, this book makes no claim to listing all the native ornamental trees and flowers—that would require a much larger volume than the present one. Probably someone's favorite species has inadvertently been omitted. But perhaps what has been written will cause gardeners to open their eyes to the beauty of our native flora, and stimulate interest in its preservation. Only those who have lived with wild flowers for a lifetime realize how rapidly this precious heritage is vanishing.

Some of the persons mentioned are internationally known authors, botanists, or horticulturists. Others are just successful gardeners, who deserve stars for their patience, perseverance, wisdom, and love of beauty. Where there is a quotation from a book, the source is given. When a well-known botanist is quoted, his title will be given in a footnote only once.

—CAROLINE DORMON

NATIVES PREFERRED

ROCK GARDENS GO NATIVE

When rock gardens had their beginning in America, not so long ago, they were planted with alpine species, alone. These dwarfs are fascinating, but growing them places this type of gardening in the category of an expensive hobby, and something for one with much leisure. But all the while there have been our native species, many of which grow happily in such situations, so why not use these "rock garden plants"?

Where I grew up there were plenty of rocks, and all my life I have played with putting them and plants together—not calling it a "rock garden," for as a child I had never heard of such a thing. The idea is prevalent that this type of gardening is impossible in the Deep South, because the delicate alpines shrivel in the heat. I wish that all the doubters could see the beautiful grounds created by Inez Conger (Arcadia) in the red clay hills of Northwest Louisiana. A good part of it is made up of brown stones which she had transported from nearby, and skillfully embedded in the hillside. Here there are cascades of *Iris cristata*, clumps of *Nemastylis*, *Phlox divaricata* in every shade, *Silenes*, masses of Violets, and many other herbaceous plants, with an occasional low Mountain Laurel for accent. Most of this is in high shade.

I wanted the delightful alpines, and tried them. Once I sent the late Mrs. DeBevoise a few native plants, then she sent me a number of her beauties. When June came, they went *out*. Carl Starker's fascinating "bushlets" met the same fate. So I decided to stay with the species that

3

TWO DWARF IRISES:
I. CRISTATA; I. VERNA

I knew could survive temperatures of a hundred and more, and there I had some surprises. The two dwarfs, *Iris verna* and *I. cristata*, are mountain plants, but I saw them growing in Central Alabama, so hopefully brought them here. After many years they are still with me, and gladden my heart each spring with their exquisite flowers, lifted only a few inches above the earth. Some gardeners complain that *I. verna* will not bloom for them, but mine give an abundance of blossoms. They are between rocks, gritty soil, on a hillside shaded from the west by tall trees.

Galax was more difficult, but I finally persuaded it to grow in full shade. Dainty *Shortia* stays with me several years, but succumbs in an unusually hot summer. To my delight, lovely *Mertensia virginica* grows happily between rocks, giving me curled racemes of pink buds and blue flowers. After flowering, the plants become too tall, but as they die off quickly, this can be endured. This beautiful flower comes back year after year, and is grown all over the Eastern United States. It has smaller relatives in mountains of the West.

The mottled leaves of Wild Ginger add beauty to any planting, and are easy and adaptable. *Asarum shuttleworthii* is the finest, with leaves marbled white and green. One of the most adaptable of wildlings is the eastern Columbine, *Aquilegia canadensis*, with its pretty ferny leaves and red-and-yellow flowers. It seems to be happy in rock gardens in almost every part of the country. Two charming plants that succeed in rock gardens in the East are Dutchman's-breeches, *Dicentra cucullaria*, and Squirrel-corn, *D. canadensis*. Both have pretty, divided leaves, and the former is decked out with cream-colored tiny pantaloons. The latter takes it name fom the fact that —alas!—squirrels and wood-mice devour the little tubers. Both want rich soil with plenty of humus. The well-known Bleeding Heart is widely grown, but is much taller and best suited for the back of the rock garden.

Most species of Phlox are easily grown and make a fine showing for a long time in spring. Probably the best known is the beautiful *Phlox divaricata*, with pretty evergreen foliage. It occurs all over the eastern part of the country, even down to Louisiana, and succeeds in gardens everywhere if given rich soil full of humus. It varies in height, and in color from pure white to light violet, and there is even a pink form (rare). I have had the white from several nurseries, but with me it is more delicate than the colored forms, and I have difficulty in keeping it. (All plants that have a tendency to die off, I keep rooting from cuttings, so I will have replacements.)

P. pilosa is easily grown in full sun, but the color most often seen is a rather hard magenta-pink. The late Ruth Dormon found a lovely almost-plumbago-blue form growing on her place at Shreveport, Louisiana, and was propagating it. Twice I have found a white one, but like other albinos it is delicate. The most beautiful of this group is one that Dr. Wherry named *P. pilosa forma ozarkana*, though it grows in sheets in Caddo Parish, Louisiana.

The flowers are a lovely soft pink, sometimes an inch across. It grows in any soil, sun or shade, and blooms over a long period in spring. There are also lavender forms, usually with a white band around the center. It is too tall for the small rock garden.

In the eastern states, *P. stolonifera* is much used in rock gardens, but the heat in Northwest Louisiana was too much for it. Harold Epstein, New York, is loud in praise of *P. stolonifera var. Blue Ridge*, a form collected and introduced by Mary G. Henry.

The numerous dwarf Phloxes of the West are tantalizing, but those that I have tried did not survive at Briarwood. Claude Barr lists *P. andicola*, a needle-leaved white, forming mats, and two others with white flowers, *P. hoodii* and *P. longifolia*, both described as low and spreading. But his favorite seems to be *P. alyssifolia*, with fragrant inch-wide flowers in both pink and white. Surely rock gardeners in the "High Prairies" avail themselves of these treasures.

Still farther West, in the Sierra Nevada and other mountains, there are delightful dwarf phloxes, such as *P. douglasii*, usually white but sometimes pink or lavender. F. O. Pearce (Orinda, California) reports that he has grown it in his garden. In the high mountain regions lucky rock-gardeners can also grow the two lovely heaths, *Phyllodoce* and *Cassiope*, low evergreen mats hung with pink or white bells.

How can anyone create a rock garden without *Phlox subulata?* Dr. Edgar Wherry says *Phlox bifida* has larger flowers, but to most gardeners it is included in *P. subulata*. The Market Bulletin women insist on calling it "Thrift." Under any name it still retains its happy disposition, accommodating itself to most any well-drained soil, in sun or shade. The tiny leaves are evergreen, so the spreading mats are attractive even in winter. In February (in the Deep South) they begin decking themselves in their pretty flowers, white, blue, lavender, and pink. They bloom for weeks, and at the height of their season form carpets of gay color.

Seldom seen in cultivation, *Ruellia ciliosa* is an attractive perennial, from six to ten inches in height. All summer it bears two-inch lavender flowers with white centers outlined in violet. The entire plant is clothed in soft ciliate hairs. It revels in loose acid soil, in full sun. It is little affected by drought.

Dainty Bloodroot is a standby in rock gardens in all the eastern states, even as far south as Louisiana if planted in a cool situation. Bloodroot and Hepatica are nearly always mentioned together as harbingers of spring, but Hepatica is more difficult where hot summers prevail. Faithful old Jack-in-the-pulpit is attractive in the shady rock garden. The leaves of both this and Bloodroot die off in summer.

It is odd that native Verbenas are not used more in sunny spots. For weeks *V. canadensis* forms sheets of lavender bloom. Moss Verbena, *V. tenuisecta*, delights us with its mats of bright color along highways, where it is kept cut low. Given the same treatment, it is charming in the rock garden. The type color is violet, but it occurs in white and pink.

In northern states, rock gardens are usually placed in full sun, but in the Deep South, they require high shade most of the day, especially in afternoon. This is the only location in which we can grow dainty *Hepatica*, also *Shortia* and *Galax*. *Trilliums*, too, like shade, and lots of humus. The handsome *T. grandiflorum*, with big white flowers, blooms one year for me, then says farewell. But Elizabeth Lawrence has it, and *T. luteum*, *T. erectum*, and *T. stylosum*, which come back year after year.

Some of the Silenes are mat-forming, and are ideal rock garden plants. *Silene wherryii* and *S. caroliniana*, with white or pink flowers, are especially lovely. Both are cold-hardy to New England, and grow happily in the Deep South if given shade. They like well-drained soil be-

ZINNIA   GRANDIFLORA;   LIGHT   YELLOW,
FORMS LOW CLUMPS.

tween rocks. It has been my experience that all *Silenes*—
except the tall *S. stellata*—are temperamental and die off
occasionally without any apparent cause. An occasional
watering with a solution (a heaping teaspoon to a gallon
of water) of Potassium permanganate helps to keep them
healthy. By crossing some of these species, Dr. Krucke-

WHITE PRAIRIE ROSE; ROSA FOLIOLOSA. (RED FRUIT)

berg (Washington State University, Seattle) has created some exquisite hybrids, with large fringed flowers. One, a lovely pink, has survived hot summers for four years, and blooms profusely.

The lower growing western *Erythroniums* are charming in cool rock gardens, but with plants as with people, it would seem that "East is East and West is West, and never the twain shall meet." Even such a famous rock gardener as Harold Epstein says, "I have a large graveyard of western plants." But John Lambert (Wixom, Mich.) says he has had the lovely *Erythronium hendersonii, E. revolutum,* and *E. oregonum* for three years, so maybe it can be done.

A plant from the western "High Prairies," *Zinnia grandiflora,* is a perfect rock garden subject. Why such a name? It does not in the least resemble a Zinnia as we know the garden plant, and the single flowers are only an inch across. It forms a low spreading plant, with branching stems only six inches high, has tiny leaves, and covers itself with soft-yellow flowers. Lorena Morgan brought me my first cut flowers from the Texas Black Lands. I still have them after five years, the form perfect, the color faded only a little. How the flower arrangers should love it! I finally wheedled a plant from Claude Barr, gave it the best substitute I could for its native soil, but it pined away. The Black Lands cover a vast area, and surely rock gardeners in this region will avail themselves of this priceless gem. An attractive companion plant is little Rock Daisy, *Melampodium,* the same size and found in the same localities. All during early summer it covers itself with tiny white "daisies."

There are two westerners that are more friendly, the lovely small roses, *Rosa foliolosa* and *R. arkansana.* The former has yellow-centered white flowers and tiny stiff shining green leaves; the latter, pink flowers and ferny foliage. Both occur in alkaline soils from Southwest Texas to the Dakotas, but also grow well here at Briarwood. *Rosa arkansana* has been grown successfully by both Mary G. Henry (Pennsylvania) and Elizabeth Lawrence (North Carolina). With the Dakotas and North Louisiana, this certainly gives it a wide range.

It is strange that small ferns are not used more between rocks, for they add a lovely softening effect. *Woodsia*, the several *Cheilanthes*, and the Spleenworts do not require much moisture and are easy to grow. I love the rock garden in winter, especially when stones have been in place long enough to gather mosses and lichens—how they gleam on a damp winter day! I pat mosses into every available space, and these thrive in shady locations.

Margaret Scruggs Carruth* prefers the term "hillside gardens," and I rather like it myself. The conception of rock gardens has so often been misconstrued and misapplied it is almost enough to prejudice one against those words. How did anyone ever get the idea that a pile of stones on level ground constituted a rock garden? The only fitting location is a hillside, the steeper the better. When I am in mountainous country, I wonder why flower lovers don't acquire sheer bluffs, and there create *real* rock gardens. Between the huge rocky outcrops grow Mountain Laurel and Wild Hydrangea, low and spreading in such situations; and almost certainly the handsome evergreen fern, *Dryopteris marginalis* will be found in shady spots. The list of delightful herbaceous plants is almost endless, and so are the possibilites for unusual

---

* Gardening in the South and West, Scruggs.

Viola rostrata; Viola papilionacae, Viola pedata.

EUSTYLIS PURPUREA.   HERBERTIA   NEMASTYLIS ACUT
                           CAERULEA.   (AND GEMINIFLOR

beauty. What fun it would be to paint a picture on the mountainside, using flowers instead of pigments!

Inez Conger even has "root gardens." In between huge gnarled roots on sides of ravines she has planted ferns and various native flowering species, and the effect is charming. Also, this serves to hold the soil.

In every region—mountains east and west, the high prairies, the sand hills—there are attractive plants perfectly suited to growing in rock gardens. In high mountains, even those in the Eastern United States, true alpines are found. From time to time, these are described in the Bulletin of the American Rock Garden Society. It is regrettable that more nurserymen do not gather seeds of our many fascinating wild flowers and put them in the trade.

Doretta Klaber has grown some of the most difficult species in her eastern rock garden. Most of these were from seed.

SUMMARY, ROCK GARDENS GO NATIVE

Iris cristata, zones 7 and 8, east. Rich soil. Shady slopes.

I. verna, 5 to 8, east. Dry slopes. Sun.

Celestials, *Nemastylis geminiflora,* 4 to 7. Heavy well
drained soil.

Phlox divaricata, 4 to 9 east of Neb. Rich soil, semi-shade.

Phlox pilosa ozarkana, 7 to 9 east of Cen. Kans. Sun.
Adaptable.

Phlox stolonifera, 6 and 7 east. Cool woodlands.

Phlox subulata, 3 to 8, east. Well drained sites, sun.
Very adaptable.

Phlox andicola, P. hoodii, P. allyssifolia, 4 to 6, west
of Minn.

Phlox douglasii, 4 to 6 west of Nebraska. Mountains.

Silene wherryii, 6 and 7, east. Shady slopes. Well drained
sites.

Silene caroliniana, 5 to 7, shade. Rich neutral soil.

Violets, many species, some in every zone except arid
regions. Semi-shade.

Galax aphylla, 7 and 8, eastern mountains. Shade.

Oconee Bells, *Shortia galacifolia,* 7 to 8, eastern mountains. Shade.

Wild Ginger, *Asarum shuttleworthii,* 6 to 8 east. Shade,
rich soil, adaptable.

Columbine, *Acquilegia canadensis,* 3 to 8 east. Shade.
Rich soil, adaptable.

Columbine, several western species, mountains.

Bleedingheart, *Dicentra eximia,* 5 to 8 east of Kansas.
Semi-shade.

Squirrel-corn, *D. canadensis,* 5 to 7 east of Nebraska.
Cool locations.

RUELLIA CILIOSA

Dutchman's Breeches, *D. cucullaria*, 3 to 7 east of Colorado. Mountains.

Phyllodoce, 3 to 5, Mts. of Pacific Coast. Tiny shrub. Acid soil.

Cassiope, 3 to 5, Mts. of Pacific Coast. Tiny shrub. Acid soil.

Bloodroot, *Sanguinaria canadensis*, 5 to 8, east. Shade. Good drainage.

Hepatica americana, 4 to 8 east. Cool shady locations.

Virginia Bluebells, *Mertensia virginica*, 3 to 8. Semi-shade. Adaptable.

Jack-in-the-pulpit, *Arasaema triphyllum*, 5 to 9. Shade. Adaptable.

Verbena canadensis, 5 to 9, east of Colo. Sun. Well drained sites.

Verbena tenuisecta (erinoides), 5 to 9. Sun. Very adaptable.

Trillium grandiflora, 4 to 7 east. Shade. *T. ovatum* in California.

T. luteum, 5 to 8 east. Cool sites, well drained.

T. erectum, 5 to 7 east, rich soil, shade.

T. stylosum, 7 to 9 east, semi-shade, rich soil.

T. undulatum, 5 to 7 east. Cool sites.

T. sessile, 4 to 9 east. *Var. californicum*, California. Rose to white.

Erythronium americanum, 3 to 9 east of Okla. Damp ground.

E. hendersonii, Oregon and Wash. Also in NE. states.

E. oregonum, Oregon and Wash. Also in NE. states.

E. revolutum, California. Cool sites, mountains.

Zinnia grandiflora, 4 to 7. High Prairies, alkaline soils.

Rock Daisy, *Melampodium*, 4 to 7, High Prairies, alkaline soils.

Rosa foliosa, 4 to 8, heavy calcareous soils, but grow in
   sand, with lime.

R. arkansana, 4 to 8, heavy calcareous soils, but will grow
   in sand with lime.

Woodsia, small ferns, some species in every zone. Steep
   shady banks.

Cheilanthes, small ferns, 5 to 8, east and west. Rocky
   ledges.

Spleenworts, *Asplenium*, some species in every zone.
   Rocky slopes.

BULBS ARE EASY

Most of our native bulbs keep their heads below ground till freezes are past, thus making their cultivation less hazardous. One of the loveliest spring flowers is *Zephyranthes atamasco*, the "Wild Easter Lily" of the South Atlantic Coast region. The common name, I think, originated at Savannah, Georgia, where the Sea Island Negroes came in with flat baskets balanced on their heads and filled with these white "lilies" and wild pink Azalea. This is around Easter, hence the name.

I do not know how far north this bulb can be grown, but Small gives it as occurring to Philadelphia. In North Carolina it forms sheets of white, and Blomquist* says the Cherokee Indians called it "Cullowhee," and it gave its lovely name to Cullowhee, North Carolina—"The Place of Lilies." Why this precious flower is not better known remains a mystery. It is not choosy as to soil, and will grow in either sun or shade. I have never seen it in a catalog, only Mrs. Ethel Harmon, Saluda, South Carolina, lists it. Years ago I got bulbs from her, and to my joy they have flourished and reseeded themselves. They grow and bloom with abandon beneath Dogwood, Silverbell, and other deciduous trees. In between my rocks—shaded from afternoon sun—they are lovely with wild Violets and small ferns. My soil is acid, sandy, and full of humus, so I fear they would not be happy in alkaline clay. The stems are seldom more than eight inches tall, each bearing one wide-open, lily-like flower, often four inches in diameter.

---

* Flowers of the South, Greene and Blomquist.

The closely related *Cooperias* (now included in *Zephyranthes* by some botanists) want quite the opposite in the way of soils, growing in sheets in the Black Lands of Texas. Both Willie Mae Kell and Margaret Carruth (Wichita Falls and Dallas) have them in their gardens. They are rather adaptable and do survive here in my acid sandy soil, but bloom only sparingly. However, for May Nichols, just two miles away, flower happily after every shower, with no attention at all. But that is in deep brownish sand, certainly on the alkaline side. There are two species, but *C. pedunculata* is much finer, with wide-open white flowers three inches across, and delicately fragrant. This valuable bulb should surely be in the trade. Along with various other *Zephyranthes* and *Habranthus*, these are known as Rain-lilies.

In Texas, too, is found the little *Habranthus texana*, bright yellow, and purplish-brown on the reverse. Though the flowers are rather small, a mass of them in bloom is an arresting sight. I have seen it occasionally around Natchitoches in Western Louisiana. Elizabeth Lawrence has it in her garden in Charlotte, North Carolina, so it can be grown far from its natural habitat. Dr Small gives two other yellow *Zephyranthes* to Texas, but these I have not known in cultivation. Mrs. Morris Clint (Brownsville, Texas), who has collected so many fine bulbous species from Mexico, gave me a lovely soft yellow *Zephyranthes* (or *Habranthus?*). The dividing line between one genus and the other is a little vague. Surprisingly, it has done well in acid, sandy soil.

The descriptions of the various *Alliums* sound delightful, but they are not for me. Only our little Wild Onion, *A. mutabile*, is happy here, growing in sandy soil, with

Buttercups and Spring Beauties. The flesh-colored flowers are small, but the fluffy heads are borne in such profusion they make a gay showing. Like all small bulbs, they should be planted by dozens to get an effect. They grow wild in rather moist meadows, but have done well in my sandy rock garden. To my surprise, Claude Barr (S. Dakota), too, says he has little success with Alliums, but Elizabeth Lawrence* is quite enthusiastic over them, though most of her species are not native.

At Wichita Falls (Texas), Willie Mae Kell grows the lovely little yellow *A. coryi*, but this is not surprising as she is in the alkaline belt, and it comes from the Texas Black Lands. Because of its low growth it is especially desirable for rock gardens, and as it is found at elevations of six thousand feet, should be hardy quite far north. I wish I knew a source for these bulbs.

How I pine for the various species of Calochortus, often referred to as the glory of California bulbs! The flowers of some are globe-shaped, giving them the delightful common name, "Fairy Lanterns." Claude Barr describes *C. gunnisoni*, Mountain Mariposa, with a lovely white chalice. He recommends *C. nuttalli*, bearing flowers of white, gold, and maroon on twelve-inch stems. In California, Charlotte Hoak grows them all, and most of them are native to that state. As Mariposa is Spanish for butterfly, the common names, Butterfly Tulips or Butterfly Lilies, seem quite fitting for these airy and exquisitely colored flowers. In the late Carl Purdy's catalog so many are described it is impossible to list them all in this book, but one of the most striking is *C. vesta*, with wide-open four-inch flowers, white, vividly shaded

---

* The Little Bulbs, Elizabeth Lawrence.

and marked with lilac and rosy-purple. Surprisingly, he found this growing in heavy clay, but for most species he recommends a sandy well drained soil.

While we are envying the West we may as well talk about *Erythroniums*, which they have there in many colors. These do not have true bulbs, but root-stocks, which spread in an odd manner. They send out side shoots and new plants are formed at the tips. Claude Barr recommends Prairie Erythronium, *E. mesochorium*, with white starry flowers tinted lavender. Small gives it as occurring from Iowa and Nebraska south to Oklahoma. But California offers the most tantalizing list. The one named for the state, *E. californicum*, bears its creamy nodding flowers in clusters, which with their richly mottled leaves form a lovely woodland picture. It likes loose gritty soil with lots of humus. *E. johnsoni*, deep rose, and *E. gigantium*, white marked brown, have exquisitely formed flowers in masses. Charlotte Hoak says, "We had acres of these."*

In the Southeast we have *Erythronium americanum*, and when its big golden stars open flat in the sun, it is something to be desired. The mottled leaves make a pretty ground-cover. Like others of the family, they must be grown in masses to achieve their full beauty. We also have *E. albidum*, but it is not to be compared with the former—even the leaves are not mottled. *Erythroniums* want loose leaf-mold with some moisture and shade.

It will be of no avail, but I must raise my voice in protest against the silly name, Dogtooth Violet. It is not related to the Violet, it does not resemble a violet,

---

* See the chapter on rock gardens.

and the only part that resembles a dog's tooth (they say) is hidden beneath the ground. The old names, Trout Lily and Adder's Tongue, are preferable, and Fawn Lily is especially lovely, for the mottled leaves suggest a little spotted fawn. But alas, people just love pointless common names, such as "English Dogwood" for Philadelphus!

There are three dainty little Iris cousins, bulbous which richly deserve wider recognition. The finest *Nemastylis geminiflora* (former *N. acuta*), holds two- to three-inch flowers on slender stems, the color frosty lavender-blue, with a white collar around the bright-yellow anthers. They look as fragile as a snowflake, and indeed they do shrivel by noon—except on cloudy days. When the sun hides his face they remain open all day. The Texas folk call them Celestials, and celestial they are. In their native habitat they grow in heavy clay, sometimes six inches deep, but they thrive and bloom here between my rocks in gritty acid soil. Elizabeth Lawrence has grown them for a long time, and, to my surprise and delight, Claude Barr writes that he, too, has had them for years. That is in Smithwick, S. Dakota, where temperatures drop to twenty below zero. When tried out in such varying climates, surely they will grow in all the states between, and much farther north. Once they could be seen in sheets in and around Shreveport, but alas, that rapidly growing city has spread over them and they are gone. Lillian Trichel found one under the edge of her house in the middle of town! Ruth Dormon grew them by hundreds from seed, flowering them the second year. But both Ruth and Lillian are gone, along with these exquisite flowers.

Eula Whitehouse* gives two species, but Small finally concluded there was only one. This is subject for debate, as they vary very much. The one with larger flowers grows much taller, to fifteen inches. Another is eight to twelve inches, with smaller flowers, but the stems branch and often show several blossoms open at the same time.

The second of these small irids is *Herbertia caerulea,* with lavender two-inch flowers intricately marked with white and dark violet on the tiny petals. The flowers are borne on six-inch stems. They are exquisite, and the first time I saw a sheet of them in a sunny meadow I almost lost my breath. Their native habitat is moist low ground near the Gulf Coast, but both Elizabeth Lawrence and I have grown them in well drained situations.

The third species is the least known of all—in fact it was lost to botanists for many years. I had known and loved it since childhood, when my parents collected and grew it at our summer home in the pine hills (where I now live). They called it Pinewoods Lily, for want of a better name, for it was not described in any botany. It is *Eustylis purpurea,* discovered by Asa Gray. The bulbs are shallow, in sandy acid soil. How well they will do in other sites I do not know, but they merit a trial. The flowers are like tiny violet Tigridias.

Camassias are charming bulbs, with their spikes of delicate light blue flowers. *C. esculenta* is very well known, but here in Northwest Louisiana we have a much smaller species better suited to rock gardens. I call it *C. hyacinthina* (Small), but am not entirely sure of its

---

* Texas Flowers, Whitehouse.

identification. It grows from six to twelve inches tall, and when massed is lovely. Occasionally a pure white one is found. These dainty things used to carpet the campus of Centenary College (Shreveport), but mowing year after year has destroyed them. Civilization is hard on wild flowers.

As a rule, Oxalis leave me cold, but our native *O. violacea* is a dear thing. The dainty pinkish-lavender flowers almost an inch across are borne on slender fleshy stems about six inches high. The few leaves, red-violet on the reverse, are ornamental. It is not invasive — as are most of its kin—but spreads slowly. It loves sandy soil and full sun and in such a situation forms a sheet of delicate beauty.

Small describes several native *Anemones*, but the only one I know is *A. caroliniana*, with starry flowers, the two rows of petals white, lavender on the reverse. Sometimes the entire flower is pinkish-lavender. These are borne singly on slender six- to ten-inch stems. When one sees a sheet of them bowing to the March wind, the sheer joy of it lifts the heart. It is not a common wild flower, but when it does occur it is en masse. It endures much neglect, but mine were finally shaded out by encroaching shrubs, for it loves sun. Small gives it as found from Nebraska to Texas and across to Georgia, Claude Barr lists it, so I see no reason why gardeners everywhere should not enjoy it. Dr. and Mrs. Julian Steyermark grow it in their wild garden at Barrington, Illinois.* Some species of Anemone may be found in almost every

---

* Wild Flowers for your Garden, Hull.

part of the United States, but none could be lovelier than this.

Among the first flowers of spring are the Buttercups, the modest wildlings related to the showy *Ranunculus* of gardens. There are many species, but my favorite is *R. apricus*, a low mat of prettily cut leaves and bright yellow flowers that glisten as if they had been shellacked. We know spring is here when we see a meadow bright with these, Blue-eyed Grass, and Spring Beauty (*Claytonia*). Often Texas "goes us one better," and she can lay claim to *R. macranthus*, with yellow flowers two inches across and with a double row of petals, sometimes as many as sixteen. An unusual feature is that the entire plant is hairy. Eula Whitehouse says it is found from Central to Southwest Texas, but surprisingly it grows well here in my acid sand. My plants were given me by Mary Lambdin, who grows it successfully in that wonderful loess at Natchez, Mississippi. It should be introduced to horticulture.

When one considers the beauty and adaptability of our larger native bulbs, it is amazing that they are not more commonly seen in gardens. Our only native Crinum, *C. americanum*, bears umbels of exquisite flowers, with long narrow segments, white, with rose stamens. Sheets of them in bloom present a charming sight. Their native habitat is low wet ground, but they bloom in my sand. They occur in the wild from Florida to Texas, and the states between should plant them freely on large grounds. It would be interesting to learn how far north they are hardy.

Hymenocallis differ from the preceding in having a staminal cup in the center. The members of this genus comprise another much neglected group. The spring-blooming species range in height from ten inches to two feet, and all have shining-green, strap-shaped leaves. The large flowers are borne in clusters, and appear with the leaves. These occur by thousands in low ground, especially in the strips between railroads and highways. *Hymenocallis rotatum* is probably the commonest species, and Small gives it as occurring from North Carolina to Florida. These thrive in gardens, if given water in the growing season, and are very attractive by pools.

The showiest member of this group is a fine species which puts up beautiful glaucous leaves in spring, which soon die off. In August the scapes arise without a leaf, bearing an umbel of very large lovely flowers, sometimes eight inches across. There are several species, but the finest is one I collected and grew for years—a nameless beauty. It has now been named *H. eulae*, honoring Dr. Eula Whitehouse, author of Texas Flowers. I shall never forget my excitement when I first saw fine clumps of it blooming in a calf pasture! This is the most adaptable species, flourishing in dry gardens, in various soils. Alas, I know of no catalog which lists it, but it can be had from the Market Bulletins, under the name, White Spider-lilies. However, these probably will not state whether spring or fall blooming, so purchaser had better inquire.

When we come to the true Lilies I will have to contradict myself, for Lilies are *not* "easy." That is, they are not easy to move from their native haunts to gardens. I first saw the magnificent *Lilium superbum* growing between rocks in the foothills of Central Alabama. I found it listed in a catalog, and ordered. Alas, I have never been able to persuade it to bloom even once for me! My conclusion is that this is due to the searing heat of our summers. It is described as "one of the easiest," which may be true in the region to which it is endemic.

To my joy, the much smaller, but lovely, *L. michauxii* (formerly *L. carolinianum*) has stayed with me at Briarwood. I did not even know that it grew in my state, but when I was taking W. W. Ashe to see *Magnolia pyramidata*, which I had discovered in Western Louisiana, I found it. While driving through Longleaf Pine woods, I whooped, "I see a red Lily!" On examining it a surprised Mr. Ashe pronounced it to be *L. michauxii*. We found others along the high, dry bank of a little stream, some with umbels of three or four flowers. I have never been able to coax more than one flower to a stem. The red-and-yellow flowers with maroon spots and very recurved segments possess a delicate perfume. Like all Lilies it is temperamental. For years I have had a clump growing on a dry bank. I tried moving some of them to a much better location—as I thought—but they did not agree with me and departed. So I put a wire pen around those remaining (to protect them from rabbits) and left them to bloom as they will.

In the eastern states are to be found *Lilium philadelphicum* and *L. grayii*, but to my taste they are much less desirable than the two preceding species. Pretty *L. canadense* is successful in the Northeastern United States, but will have none of my hot summers. My favorite of the native Lilies is *L. catesbaei*, but I have never known it to succeed in a garden. The late David Fischer had it in his natural bog, and gave me a plant. It was kind enough to bloom for me, so I could paint it for Wild Flowers of the Deep South, then a severe freeze got it. The same thing happened to three given me by Mrs. Fred Taylor, taken from her wild garden in South Mississippi. So this is a warning: only those who own a natural bog near the Gulf Coast can grow this lovely thing. Alas, its bright-red upward-facing flowers tempt gardeners, but when they yield they only hasten its extermination.

Of the western Lilies, Carl Purdy listed in his catalogs *Lilium humboldtii* and *L. washingtonianum*, both magnificent species with big umbels of showy flowers. I have seen the brilliant *L. pardalinum* offered in other catalogs. I have no information as to these species being grown successfully in the East, so with the Lilies, as with many other groups of plants, it is wise to confine ourselves to species native to a region.

NATIVES PREFERRED 31

SUMMARY, BULBS ARE EASY

Zephyranthes atamasco, 7 to 9 e. of Cen. Tex. Most any
acid soil.

Cooperia pedunculata, 6 to 8, Tex. and La. Heavy soil.
Sun or semi-shade.

Habranthus texana, 7 to 9, Tex. to N. C. Heavy soil. Sun.

Allium mutabile, 7 to 9, e. Tex. to n. Fla. Various soils
and sites.

Allium coryii, 6 to 8 west. Dry sites. Neutral soil.

Mountain Mariposa, *Calochortus gunnisonii.* Rocky
Mts. Humus.

Calochortus vesta, 4 to 6, Mts. of Cal., and Northeastern
states. Clay soil.

Calochortus nuttallii, 4 and 5, w. of Minn. Light soil,
humus.

Erythronium mesochorium, 4 to 6, w. of Wis.

Erythronium californicum, Mts. of Cal., but has been
grown in Ne. Gritty soil.

Erythronium johnsonii and *E. giganteum,* Mts. of Cal.
Humus.

Erythronium americanum, Fawn Lily, 4 to 9 e. of Okla.
Damp ground, acid.

Celestials, *Nemastylis geminiflora,* 4 to 8 e. of Colo. Dry
soil. Adaptable.

Herbertia caerulea, 7 to 9 east. Low damp ground, acid.

Eustylis purpurea, probably 7 to 9 e. of Cen. Tex. Dry,
loose, acid soil.

Camassia esculenta, 5 to 8 east and west. Well drained
soil, adaptable.

Camassia hyacinthina, 7 to 8, La. and Tex., probably
  other states. Dry.

Oxalis violacea, 4 to 9, many states. Dry soil. Sun or shade.
  Adaptable.

Buttercup, *Ranunculus apricus,* 4 to 8, widespread. Low
  ground. Sun.

Hairy Buttercup, *R. macranthus,* 8, Tex. to Miss., probably other states.

Spring Beauty, *Claytonia virginica,* 5 to 9, e. Damp
  ground. Adaptable.

Crinum americanum, 8 and 9, Fla. to Tex. Low rich soil.
  Adaptable.

Spiderlily, *Hymenocallis,* many species, Fla. to N. C.
  Adaptable.

August Spiderlily, *H. eulae,* 8 and 9, Tex. to Fla. Very
  adaptable.

Lilium superbum, 4 to 7 e. of Kans. Cool sites, semi-
  shade. Rich, dry soil.

Carolina Lily, *L. michauxii,* 7 to 9, e. of Cen. Tex. Dry
  soil, shade.

Lilium canadensis, 4 to 8, northern sts. e. of Neb. Damp
  ground.

Lilium philadelphicum, 4 to 7 east. Cool sites. Well
  drained soil.

Lilium grayii, 6, Northern sts., or mountains in S., East
  of Neb.

Lilium catesbaei, 7 to 9, e. of Tex. Wet ground. Sun.

Lilium humboldtii, Mts. of California.

Lilium washingtonianum, Oregon and Mts. of Cal.

Lilium pardalinum, Mts. of Cal., and probably other sts.
  Adaptable.

THE SHADY TRAIL

It is surprising how many native plants will grow and bloom in shade. The finest display of Cardinal Flower I ever saw was a natural planting, in rather low ground beneath trees. There were hundreds of beautiful blazing spikes, scattered over a rather large area.

My favorite walk is down a hill, along a winding path between my house and the pond. It twists and dips and rises, with an occasional shrub, and around that a new vista. Where there is a sudden small drop, one or two flat brown rocks have been sunk to serve as steps. Here native Azaleas have done well, with watering only during extreme droughts. There is one low clump of Mountain Laurel, very vigorous and happy. Oakleaf Hydrangea does well here, in fact the flowers are whiter and prettier when grown in shade.

This is the place for Jack-in-the-pulpit, Mayapple, and Trilliums. Trilliums must have shade and humus. *Phlox divaricata* is lovely here—if you do not have rabbits. In winter it forms mats of green, and in spring sends up numerous clusters of lavender-blue. For an occasional spot of gay red, Pinkroot, *Spigelia marilandica*, is very effective. And brilliant Oswego Tea, *Monarda didyma*, also likes shade. Clumps of native Columbines should be placed near the trail, so their delicate beauty can be appreciated. *Mertensia virginica*, with its curling racemes of pink buds and blue flowers, is lovely, especially between rocks. Thalictrums, with their ferny leaves, are attractive when massed.

And how ferns revel in shade! Certainly one of the most beautiful is the native Maidenhair, *Adiantum peda-*

A RUSTIC BRIDGE ACROSS A LITTLE STREAM, WITH MASSES OF WILD FLOWERS. THE CONGER GARDEN, IN HILLS OF NORTH LOUISIANA.

tum. The slender shining black stems hold up parasols of delicate foliage. It is adaptable and very easy to grow, if given plenty of humus. As they will be growing under deciduous trees, leaves will fall, and these should be allowed to lie and decay. An overly neat wild garden is not a happy one. Most all species, except the bog ferns, will thrive in such situations. As the lovely Maidenhair, and many others, are deciduous, the evergreen Christmas fern, with the burdensome name, *Polystichum acrostichoides*, should be freely used. It prefers rich soil, but will grow most anywhere if given shade and humus. It is perfectly hardy, and is found from Canada to Florida and Louisiana. Shieldfern, *Dryopteris marginalis*, is a beautiful evergreen species, hardy, but not quite as easy to grow as the preceding. In the north and east, two dainty evergreen ferns, *Polystichum lonchitis* and *P. braunei*, thrive in shady spots. They cannot endure the heat of summer in the Deep South.

Clumps of *Iris cristata* and *Asarum shuttleworthii* are lovely, and little *Mitchella repens* will carpet the ground between larger plants. Fragrant Carolina Lily, *L. michauxii*, will grow in shade, and so will dainty Shooting-stars. North and east, *Campanula rotundifolia* and *Cimicifuga racemosa* must have a place on the shady trail. Harebells (*Campanula*) hang over steep slopes most entrancingly, swinging their tiny blue bells. Cimicifuga should not be planted in front of low-growing plants, for the white spires tower to six feet, but are beautiful showing up behind low evergreens. Two of these evergreens can be *Pieris lucida* and *Leucothoe catesbaei*, for they thrive in shade, north or south. Tiarella and Heuchera bear sprays of dainty flowers, and the leaves color

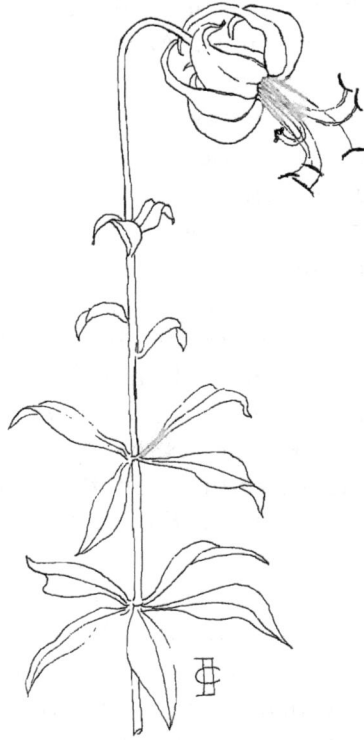

CAROLINA LILY; LILIUM MICHAUXII.

beautifully in fall. Of course there will be Violets all
along the shady trail, for they will bloom with just the
sunlight that sifts down through tall trees.

Solomon's Seal, Bloodroot, and Hepatica love sifted
sun and shadow. North and East, Galax, with its pretty
bronzy leaves, may be added, and dainty Shortia. And

these lucky gardeners can also have the two charming Dicentras, Squirrel-corn and Dutchman's Breeches.

In the West, such a situation calls for the several beautiful Erythroniums, and their lovely blue Columbines. For Washington and Oregon, Carl Starker is enthusiastic over *Vaccinium vitis-idaea*, which forms evergreen mats in either sun or shade. It will carpet steep banks, and with its pink flowers, followed by red berries, is a charming sight. As it belongs to the Heath Family, of course it demands acid soil.

South, North and East, on the lower reaches of the trail, Closed Gentians will gladden November days with their beautiful blue. And up-and-down all the length of the trail, graceful Wreath Goldenrod and the small-flowered late Asters will wreathe banks in delicate beauty.

Leucothoe catesbaei.

SUMMARY, THE SHADY TRAIL

Mountain Laurel, *Kalmia latifolia,* 5 to 8 and n. 9 e.,
    slopes. Acid soil.

Hydrangea quercifolia, 7 to 9 e. Slopes. Acid soil. Adapta-
    ble. Shrub.

Cardinal Flower, *Lobelia cardinalis,* 3 to 9 e. of Cen. Tex.
    Moist sites.

Jack-in-the-pulpit, *Arisaema triphyllum,* 5 to 9 e. of Colo.
    Moist ground.

Mayapple, *Podophyllum peltatum,* 3 to 9 e. of Neb. Light
    rich soil.

Trilliums, many sp., northern states and cool regions of
    upper South.

Phlox divaricata, 4 to 9 e. of Neb. Rich soil, semi-shade.
    Adaptable.

Pinkroot, *Spigelia marilandica,* 6 to 9 e. of Cen. Okla.
    Rich soil.

Monarda didyma, 3 to 8 e. Rich soil. Shade, except in
    mountains.

Columbine, *Aquilegia canadensis,* 3 to 8 e. Slopes, semi-
    shade. Rich soil.

Aquilegia, western species, mountains of the West.

Virginia Bluebells, *Mertensia virginica,* 3 to 8 e. Gritty
    soil.

Thalictrum polygamum, 3 to 9 e. of Ill. Other sp. widely
    distributed.

Maidenhair Fern, *Adiantum pedatum,* 3 to 8, cool sites.
    Not in arid reg.

Christmas Fern, *Polystichum acrostichoides,* 4 to 9 e. of
    Neb. Slopes.

LEUCOTHOE RECURVA; TALL SHRUB; DECIDUOUS.

PIERIS NITIDA (LYONIA NITIDA); LOW EVERGREEN.

Shield Fern, *Dryopteris marginalis,* 3 to 8 e. of Neb. Shady slopes.

Polystichum lonchitis, northern states. Well drained sites. Shade.

P. braunei, northern states. Well drained sites. Shade.

Iris cristata, 7 and 8 e. Rocky slopes. Shade. Rich soil.

Wild Ginger, *Asarum shuttleworthii,* 6 to 8 e. Well drained shady sites.

Partridgeberry, *Mitchella repens,* 4 to 9 e. of Neb. Dry acid soil. Shade.

Carolina Lily, *Lilium michauxii,* 7 and 8 e. of Okla. Acid or neutral.

Shootingstars, *Dodecatheon,* some sp. in every zone except arid regions.

Hairbells, *Campanula rotundifolia,* northern states, s. to mts. of 7.

Cimicifuga racemosa, 3 to 7 e. of Minn. C. americana, eastern mountains.

Tiarella cordifolia, 3 to 8 e. Light soil, slopes. Other sp. in other zones.

Heuchera americana, 3 to 8 e. of Neb. Adaptable. Other sp. in other zones.

Violets, some species in every zone except arid regions.

Solomons seal, *Polygonatum biflorum,* 3 to 9 e. of Kans. Light soil. Slopes.

Bloodroot, *Sanguinaria canadensis,* 5 to 8 e. Light soil, shade.

Hepatica americana, 4 to 8 e. Shady slopes. Light neutral soil.

Troutlilies, *Erythroniums,* northwestern states. Abundant humus.

Galax aphylla, 7 and 8 e. of Okla. Slopes, dry soil, acid or neutral.

FOUR TRILLIUMS: 1. T. LUTEUM. 2. T. LUDOVICIANUM. 3. T. GRANDIFLORUM. 4. T. STYLOSUM.

Oconee Bells, *Shortia galacifolia,* 7 and 8 e. of Tex. Cool
   slopes.
Dutchman's Breeches, *Dicentra cucullaria,* 3 to 7 e. of
   Colo. Cool slopes.
Squirrelcorn, *D. canadensis,* 5 to 7 e. of Neb. Cool slopes.
Closed Gentian, *Gentiana andrewsii,* 4 to 7, e. of Neb.
   Moist ground.
Sou. Closed Gentian, *G. saponaria,* 5 to 9 e. of Kans.
   Moist acid ground.
Wreath Goldenrod, *Solidago rugosa,* 5 to 9 e. of Cen. Tex.
   Some sp. all zones.
Wreath Asters, *Aster latiflorus, A. undulatus, A. drum-*
   mondii, 5 to 9 e. There are some sp. of Aster in every
   zone, usually on rather dry slopes.
Pieris lucida (Lyonia nitida) , 7 to 9 e. of Okla. Moist
   acid soil.
Leucothoe Catesbaei, 7 and 8 e. of Tex. Damp acid soil,
   shade.

WILD AND SUNNY

In prairie country in spring and summer, one sees wild gardens at their finest. The color combinations are ravishing: the clear pink of Sabbatia with bright blue of Larkspur and sulphur yellow of Evening Primroses; Indian Paintbrush with Bluebonnets; Penstemons in various colors with dainty white Lazy Daisy; sheets of Gaillardia in gay red and yellow; and many others. But to attempt to dig these beauties and carry them to gardens is simply destroying them. Seed is the answer. Many can be purchased from wild flower nurseries, others can be collected.

Anyone with sufficient space and sun can have sheets of color with wild flowers. But no mowing! Many of the species described are either perennials or biennials and do not bloom the first year from seed. If planted as soon as mature, seeds germinate quickly and form pretty little green tufts, which survive severe winter weather. Some annuals, such as *Rudbeckia hirta*, do the same thing. Weeding, if any, must be done by hand. But with the delight of seeing seedlings come into flower the second spring or summer, no amount of trouble is too much, and gardening takes on a new meaning.

Among the following list of plants, some require alkaline soil. This is usually heavy and tight, and spading in some humus helps seedlings to take hold while young. Some sandy soils are on the alkaline side, as in parts of Florida, and in this Lupines will flourish. This is also what *Penstemon murrayanus* (red) likes. Where very acid conditions exist, crushed limerock or basic slag may be purchased, spread liberally, and spaded in. Of course

ECHINACEAE PALLIDA.   POPPY MALLOW:

(PINK. PERENNIAL)   CALLIRHOE PAPAVER.

this will gradually leach out, and have to be renewed
every two or three years.

Happily, a number of native plants are so adaptable
they will grow in almost any type of soil. One of these
is Pale Coneflower, *Echinacea pallida*, ranging in color
from pinkish-lavender to rose. The flowers are so much

more graceful than the heavier *E. purpurea*, sold by nurseries as *Rudbeckia purpurea*. Another is pretty *Oenothera
speciosa*, forming sheets of pink and white all spring and
early summer. Wild Larkspurs, *Delphinium*, will thrive
in various situations, and their spikes of bright blue add
a happy touch to the blanket of color. Gayfeathers, *Liatris*, are so easy to grow, and come in shades of lavender,
and sometimes pure white. Amsonia, several species, bear
their panicles of light blue flowers in spring, and are
happy in either full sun or part shade. Spiderworts deserve a place in any wild garden, especially the western
species, *Tradescantia bracteata*. It comes in every shade
of blue, pink, deep rose, and pure white. They begin
blooming when stems are only a few inches above the
ground, but gradually get taller as the season advances.
If spent stems are cut off, they flower over at least three
months. Baptisias, with racemes of yellow or white, seem
to be little known, but are very attractive. Once established, clumps come back from roots year after year.

The dainty Shooting-stars, *Dodecatheon*, are easily
grown from seed, and a sheet of them in flower is an unforgettable sight. They are perennial, but leaves die off
early, so it is advisable to mark the site so as not to dig
into them while dormant. The several lavender *Monardas*
thrive in full sun, but the red *M. didyma* prefers shade.
Goldenrods and native Asters are lovely in the sunny
garden, but as most of them are rather tall they should
be placed in the background.

Some native plants demand alkaline soil, and will grow
in nothing else. One of these is the beautiful Texas Bluebell (*Eustoma*), and another is *Eryngium leavenworthii*.
Poultry manure is alkaline, so I spaded up a spot where a

chicken house had stood and planted the Eryngium there. It flourished and bloomed, so that is one way to have this wonderful plant. But chicken manure is strong, so should be used rather sparingly. Most of the lovely prairie flowers like alkalinity, but as prairies cover a vast region, wild gardens in this area should be easy.

Some species of the plains grow in wooded sand hills, as well, and if given plenty of sunlight will respond with colorful masses of bloom. *Sabbatias*, with their clear bright pink, are among the most entrancing of wild flowers, but difficult. Scattering seed in favorable spots is the only way to acquire them. Most species are biennials, and the first year form flat rosettes of roundish leaves. The second year stems arise with many slender branches, each tipped with a showy flower.

Scarlet *Gilia* is another biennial that does not bloom till the second year. Seeds should be scattered liberally as soon as they mature. The smaller blue *Gilias* of the prairies are lovely, but require alkaline soil. Poppy Mallows, *Callirhoe papaver* and *C. involucrata*, have pretty little rounded leaves the first year. The second, they branch, bearing showy "Wine-cups" on long stems. They form carrot-like roots and come back year after year. But gophers love them, so if they come, put poisoned grain in the runs. (Cover with a weight so birds cannot get it.)

Salvia azurea is a perennial and persists for years. But bright-red *S. coccinea* is an annual and has to be re-planted each year. However, it re-seeds itself, and one soon has a plentiful supply of plants. Both these Salvias bloom all summer. S. azurea grows tall, and should be pinched back to keep it low and branching. *Helianthus*

WESTERN EVENING PRIMROSE;
CENOTHERA RHOMBIPETALA.

WINTER HUCKLEBERRY; VACCIN
ARBOREUM. SHRUB OR LOW TI

and the *Rudbeckias* bloom the second year from seed, and keep the wild garden gay with bright yellow through summer and fall. All the native *Verbenas* and *Phloxes* are easy to grow, and give us lovely carpets of bright lavender.

Nearly all of the species listed are quite hardy. Coral-bean, *Erythrina herbacea*, should survive in cold regions, for the tremendous root goes deep. Its tall spires of bright crimson flowers are striking, and these are followed by brown beans that open to display scarlet seeds. These hold their color indefinitely and are attractive in dried arrangements. In Southwest Louisiana it is known as Mamou. Butterfly Weed, *Asclepias tuberosa,* is another with a deep root, so should be fairly coldproof. No wild garden is complete without the lovely sparkling blue of Dayflower, both *Commelina Crispa* and *C. angustifolia.* Some of my gardening friends say "no" when I offer Commelina, for they are acquainted with *C. communis,* only, the wretched weed that is such a pest. The exquisite butterfly-flowers of the two above are the very spirit of a summer morning.

A low shrubby perennial, *Ceanothus americanus,* adds a happy touch of fluffy white, and is hardy to Canada. Its common names are Jersey Tea and Redroot. White *Penstemons,* too, are lovely in the sunny garden, though they will grow and bloom in high shade. I wonder why Prickly Poppy, *Argemone alba,* is not seen more often? Its big silky white flowers are borne freely all spring and summer, and even the spiny white-and-green leaves are pretty. Californians have the lovely Castillija Poppy, *Romneya coulteri,* with its huge white flowers. It has been grown in other states, and is worthy of a trial. Rex Pearce offers seed. Another perennial with fringed white flowers is *Silene stellata,* about two feet high, and blooming in early summer.

The native Hibiscus, white, pink, yellow, and red, are beautiful and very easy to grow. They bloom the second year from seed. Shrubby perennials, they die to the ground in winter. They are usually found growing in low damp ground, but are very adaptable, and thrive in almost any location. Rose Mallow, *H. moscheutos*, can be grown to the Dakotas.

If the gardener *must* hasten matters, plants of many of these beauties can be purchased from nurseries dealing in native species. If roots are dry when they arrive, the entire plant should be submerged in water for about an hour, then planted at once. If watered well and shaded for a few days, they will recover from the shock of being moved. In mild climates, fall and winter are best for transplanting. Where the ground remains frozen for long periods, early spring is better.

The best friend of the wild garden is humus. Prepared compost is fine, but well rotted leaves and grass clippings will serve. When I see people burning piles of oak leaves, I want to cry out, "Don't!" for there is no better soil-conditioner. Surely every gardener has some hidden spot where leaves can be dumped in a hole, weighted with a little soil, and allowed to decay. Humus spread several inches deep, then thoroughly spaded in loosens soil that is too tight. For poor sandy land it is a necessity, for it enriches it and helps to retain moisture. For acid-loving plants, a little cotton-seed-meal can be added to poor soils. If they want alkalinity, bone-meal should be used. Sawdust that has been exposed to the weather for several years makes an excellent mulch.

By adding Mistflower *Eupatorium coelestinum*, the Goldenrods, the several Liatris, and the many Asters, the sunny wild garden can be a gay affair till into late fall.

SUMMARY, WILD AND SUNNY

Texas Bluebonnet, *Lupinus texensis*, 5 to 9. Sand, neutral
or alkaline. Sun.

Lupinus diffusus, 7 to 9 e. Deep sand. Sun. Neutral soil.

L. perennis, 5 to 9 e. Deep sand. Sun. Neutral soil.

Penstemon digitalis, 4 to 9, prob. e. and w. Very adaptable. Sun or shade.

P. murrayanus, Tex. and La. prob. other sts. Deep sand,
on alkaline side.

Pale Coneflower, *Echinaceae pallida*, 4 to 9. Dry soil.
Very adaptable. Sun.

Oenothera speciosa, 5 to 9, Ariz. to N. C. Very adaptable.

Delphinium carolinianum, 6 to 9. Dry soil. Adaptable.
Sun.

Liatris, some species in all zones s. of 3. Adaptable. Dry
soil. Sun.

Amsonia, 5 to 9 e. of Colo. Several species. Rich soil.
Adaptable.

Spiderworts, *Tradescantia bracteata*, 6 to 9, east of Neb.
Adaptable.

Shootingstars, *Dodecatheon*, some species in zones from
4 s. Rich soil. Sun.

Bergamot, *Monarda fistulosa*, 5 to 9. Dry soil, in many
states. Adaptable.

Texas Bluebell, *Eustoma russellianum*, Texas, probably
other states. Alkaline.

Eryngium leavenworthii, 7 to 9 w. Heavy alkaline soil.
Sun.

Lazy Daisy, *Aphanostephus skirrobasis*, 7 and 8. Prairies,
heavy dry soil.

Blanketflower, *Gaillardia pulchella*, 4 to 8 w. Dry soil.
   Prairies.
Sabbatia angularis, 4 to 9 e. of Cen. Tex. Heavy dry soil.
   Sun.
S. dodecandra, 5 to 9 e. Moist ground. Sun.
Scarlet Gilia, *Gilia rubra*, 7 to 9 e. of Cen. Tex. Sandy
   soil. Sun.
Poppy Mallow, *Callirhoe involucrata*, 4 to 9 e. Dry sites.
   Sun.
Poppy Mallow, *C. papaver*, 7 and 8 e. Dry sandy soil,
   acid. Sun.
Prickly Poppy, *Argemone alba*, 7 and 8 prob. others. Dry
   sandy soil. Sun.
Castillija Poppy, *Romneya coulteri*. California, prob.
   other states.
Salvia azurea, 7 to 9, Prob. many states. Dry acid soil.
   Sun.
S. coccinea, 7 to 9 e. Rich soil, but adaptable. Sun or
   semi-shade.
Helianthus angustifolius, 7 to 9, acid soil. Very adaptable.
Rudbeckia hirta, 7 to 9 e. Dry acid soil. Sun.
R. triloba, 7 to 9 e. of Cen. Tex. Very adaptable. Sun.
Coralbean, *Erythrina herbacea*, 7 to 9, E. of Cen. Tex.
   Dry sandy soil.
Dayflower, *Commelina angustifolia*, 7 to 9, E. of Cen.
   Tex.
Dayflower, *Commelina crispa*, 5 to 9, Colo. to Tenn. Dry
   sandy soil.
Jersey Tea, *Ceanothus americanus*, 4 to 9, E. of Kans.
   Dry sandy soil.
Silene stellata, 4 to 9, E. of Kans. Various soils, acid or
   neutral.

Hibiscus, a number of sp., mostly southern. Shrubby
  perennials.
Rose Mallow, *H. moscheutos,* 3 to 9, E. of Dakotas.
  Shrubby perennial.
Mistflower, *Eupatorium coelestinum,* 5 to 9 E. of Colo.
  Very adaptable.
Goldenrods, *Solidago,* some sp. in every zone. Adaptable.
Wild Asters, some sp. in every zone. Very adaptable.
Butterfly Weed, *Asclepias tuberosa,* 3 to 9, E. and W.
  Very adaptable.

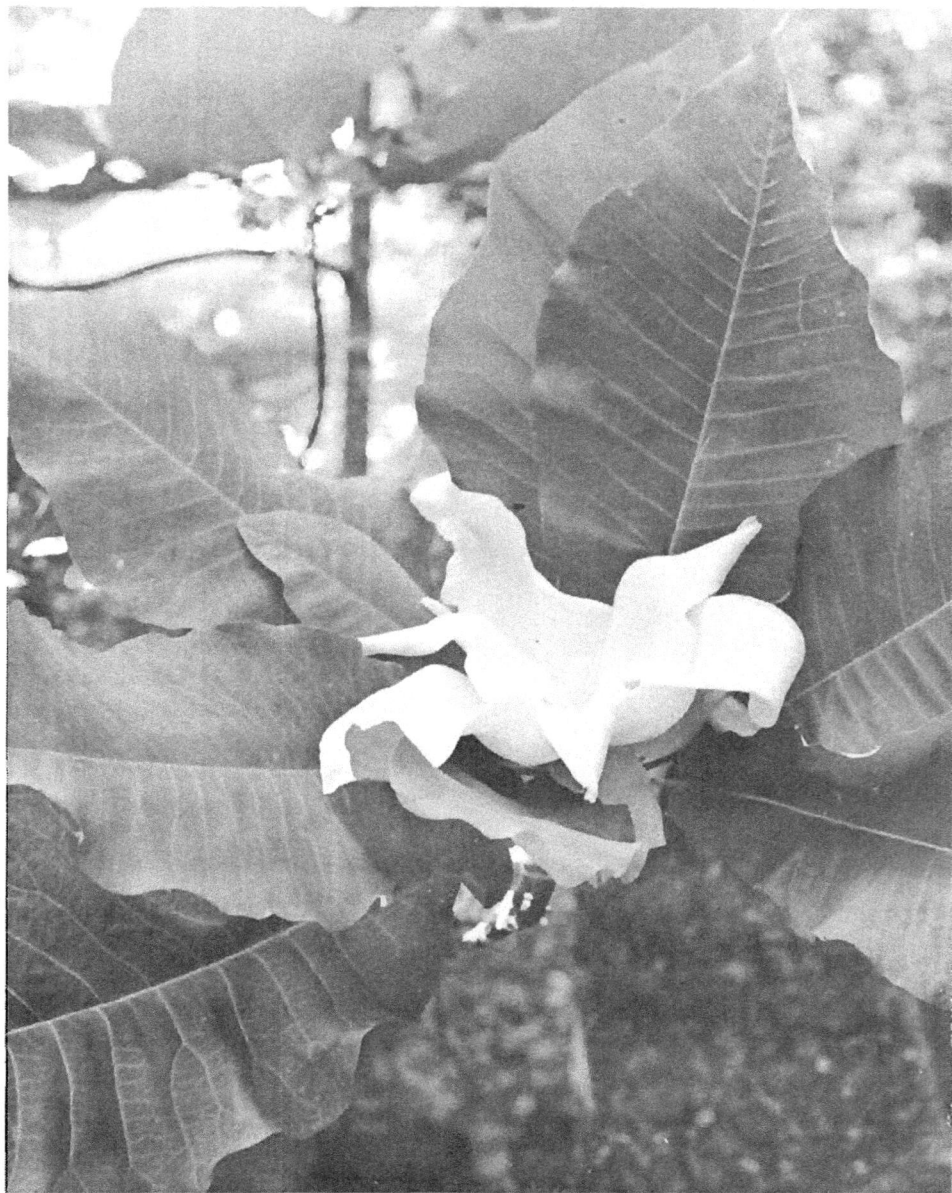

MAGNOLIA MACROPHYLLA; WITH SIXTEEN-
INCH FLOWERS. "THE MOST SPECTACU-
LAR FLOWERING TREE IN THE TEMPERATE
ZONE."

FLOWERING TREES AND SHRUBS

All trees bear flowers of some kind, but the term "flowering trees" is commonly used to designate those whose blossoms are showy, very fragrant, or otherwise interesting. America is truly blessed with trees and shrubs of this type. China, alone, can claim a greater number of ornamental species.

Of all these, the Magnolias must take first rank. It is true that some of them cannot be grown in parts of the country where below-zero temperatures hold for long periods, but in the South and on the Pacific Coast they should certainly be given a place in any planting where space permits. They prefer a deep loose soil, mildly acid, but are remarkably adaptable. When given plenty of humus and water, they respond gratefully, but after they get well started will survive during droughts.

Magnolia grandiflora should be crowned queen of trees. The shining evergreen leaves, alone, should give it a place of honor in the garden; and when the ten-inch creamy-white flowers tip the branches it is almost overwhelming. From April till late July, they fill the air with their rich perfume. It occurs in the wild from North Carolina to Florida, but has been successfully grown as far north as Pennsylvania. It comes through zero temperatures unscathed.

The semi-evergreen *Magnolia virginiana*, Sweet Bay, is not so showy as its better known sister, but is lovely nevertheless. The light green leaves are silvery-white on the reverse and are charmingly displayed in a high wind. East of the Mississippi River the flowers are only about 2½ inches across, and borne on small trees. But in

55

western Louisiana and eastern Texas there is a variety which attains a height of 70 feet, and which bears flowers 5 inches in diameter. Both are found in sandy bogs, but astonishingly, will grow almost anywhere. I know of one in Shreveport, Louisiana, which is thriving on a claybank. The creamy-white flowers fill the whole surrounding air with delightful perfume.

The two Magnolias just described will flourish in various situations, in almost any soil except tight alkaline clay. But the deciduous species are more difficult. The finest of these is *Magnolia macrophylla*, with sixteen-inch flowers nestling in whorls of yard-long leaves. It is most beautiful when viewed from the top of a bluff, for branches are uplifted, with a huge flower at the tip of each. The Englishman, J. G. Millais,* calls it "the most spectacular flowering tree in the Temperate Zone." It must start life in high shade, but it soon shoots up, reaching for the light. It it is difficult to transplant, and only small ones should be attempted. In fact, the surest way to acquire it is to grow it from seed. Like all Magnolia seeds, these have an oily covering which must be thoroughly washed off. Covered lightly, they germinate in a short while. Given a deep, light, rich soil, *Magnolia macrophylla* grows very rapidly, and a gardener will feel richly rewarded for any amount of trouble taken in growing this magnificent tree. It is found occasionally from Kentucky to Florida and Louisiana, but can be grown much farther north.

Magnolia fraseri and *M. pyramidata* are much smaller trees, with attractive leaves and cream-white seven-inch flowers. Their value is that they will come into

---

* Magnolias, J. G. Millais.

flower when not more than three feet tall, and seldom reach a height of more than 20 feet. The rose-red fruits, about 2 inches long, are as ornamental as the blossoms. These two are rather difficult, and should be attempted on cool hillsides, only.

While not so showy as some species, *Magnolia acuminata* is easy to grow, and eventually becomes a rather large handsome tree. The tulip-shaped flowers are yellowish-green, and sometimes clear yellow. The oblong light-green leaves fall in autumn.

Tulip Tree, *Liriodendron tulipifera*, is a closely related species which deserves to be better known. The pretty lobed leaves are unique, for they look as if they had been sheared off near the tip, while the flowers resemble tulips, greenish-yellow, with bright orange markings. Like *Magnolia grandiflora*, it will grow in sand hills or in alluvial soils, and there is no finer street tree. It must be given plenty of space in which to reach and spread, for it attains magnificent proportions. Branches should be allowed to grow low, the better to display the pretty flowers. The most attractive specimen I ever saw sheltered a big spring on a rocky hillside in Alabama.

A "lost tree," or rather a large shrub, is *Magnolia cordata*, with rather broad leaves, heart-shaped at the base, and small, cupped, clear yellow flowers. It was discovered by Nuttall, lost, then rediscovered by Berckmans, who introduced it to horticulture. It must be growing in some old gardens around Augusta, Georgia, and it is to be hoped that some possible owner will permit it to be re-introduced once more.

A related shrub, Star Anise, *Ilicium floridanum*, is most attractive, but occurs in the Gulf States, only, from

1. Tulip Tree; Liriodendron tulipifera.
2. Sweet Bay; Magnolia virginiana.
3. Cucumbertree; Magnolia acuminata.

Florida to Louisiana. The leathery oblong leaves are evergreen, and are strongly aromatic when bruised. The odd spidery flowers are velvety crimson, about 2 inches across. This pretty shrub likes high shade and a light soil rich in humus. I do not know how far north it is hardy, but it has not been damaged by zero temperatures.

In spring, smaller trees and large shrubs give us our floodtide of blossoming, beginning in early March with the Shadblows and Wild Plums. The Shadblows vary in size from a low shrub, *Amalanchier stolonifera*, to a tree, *A. laevis*, which may become 40 feet in height. The racemes (usually drooping) of feathery white flowers come with the delicately colored unfolding leaves, a lovely combination. *Amalanchier canadensis* varies greatly, some becoming small trees, others flowering freely when large shrubs. A number of species are offered in catalogs, *A. sanguinea* and *A. laevis* being described as the most attractive, but I have not succeeded with these two here in North Louisiana. All species seem very adaptable as to soils and sites, requiring little care.

There are many Wild Plums, and all are most attractive. *Prunus americana*, east of the Mississippi River, and *P. mexicana* to the west, are fairly large spreading trees, bearing loose clusters of white flowers in the wintry woods. The fruits, from light red to purple, ripen in late summer or fall, and when fully ripe are fragrant and palatable. The Sloes, *P. umbellata*, come a little later, the tight panicles of smaller flowers are borne so closely they form soft banks of snowy bloom. The trees are low and rounded, and in late summer the branches droop to the ground with their burden of small fruits, shading

SLOE (PRUNUS UMBELLATA) IS A MASS OF SNOW IN SPRING. IN LATE SUMMER THE SMALL FRUITS—PINK, RED AND PURPLE—WEIGH DOWN THE BRANCHES.

from pink to purple. No one seems to plant these charm-
trees—another horticultural mystery!

Of course the flowering of Dogwood, *Cornus florida*,
is the hightide of spring. Where they get the right
amount of sunlight, these graceful trees whiten the hillsides, forming an unforgettable picture. It is truly an
American tree, and should be made the national flower.
It is told that an Englishman, visiting American gardens,
looked wistfully at their snowy display all over the coun-
tryside, then remarked, "Give me your dogwoods and
you may have all the rest!"

Dogwoods are a little difficult in gardens, but once
established, flower more profusely than in the wild. They
like a loose soil, acid, and full of humus. They abhor
drought, and if there are no rains in July and August,
refuse to put on buds for next spring. Some years ago,
we had three terrible droughts in succession, and almost
every big dogwood at Briarwood died. The young trees
stood up much better, and now meet over the drive. If
one must have a spotless lawn, don't plant these beloved
trees, for they must be mulched until branches reach out
and shade the spread of roots. The old adage was never
truer than in the case of growing dogwoods, for small
plants are much easier to get established, so, "'haste
makes waste." For some reason, *Cornus florida rubra*
refuses to grow for me. It evidently prefers a soil con-
taining more minerals, for the finest specimens I have
seen were in alluvial soil.

On the West Coast, flower lovers enjoy the very fine
Cornus nuttallii, with six-inch flowers and red fruits, and
which sometimes reaches a height of seventy feet. Alas,
it has failed with me, along with other western plants. I

know of no one who has grown it successfully in the Eastern States. It failed at the Arnold Arboretum.

The flowering of dainty Fringe Tree, *Chionanthus virginica*, overlaps that of dogwood. The name is truly descriptive, for the blossoms form a delicate fringe, filling the woods with misty white. It begins to bloom when only a few feet tall, but eventually becomes a small tree. It has a mat of fine roots, and is much more easily transplanted than Dogwood—*if* those roots are not allowed to dry out for one minute. The drooping panicles of blue fruits are beautiful, but unfortunately—like the hollies—staminate and pistillate flowers are borne on separate trees, so not all produce berries. There is compensation, however, for male flowers have longer fringes and are more showy.

Why does no one plant the Hawthorns? These low spreading trees are beautiful both in flower and fruit, and with a hundred species, some of them may be grown anywhere. Naturally, only a few of these can be described in these pages, but their variety is almost endless. Washington Thorn, Parsley Haw, and Spatulate-leaved Haw have prettily cut leaves, and masses of small brilliant-red fruits in winter. The first is the only one I have seen advertised by a nursery. The many species in the Crus-galli group have thick, shining, undivided leaves, masses of white flowers, and either red or yellow fruits. These are found growing in heavy clay, on the alkaline side, but are very adaptable. One of the loveliest of the family, *Crataegus drymophila*, is found in the sand hills. The flowers of most haws appear after the leaves, but the dainty blooms of this one come with unfolding leaves, which are flesh-colored, and the combination is exquisite. Anyone with fairly low ground can grow the May-haw, *Crataegus aestivales,* which, astonishingly, ripens, delicious red fruits in late April. These haws are gathered in quantities for the making of jelly. One of the most interesting of the group is *Crataegus brachyacantha,* which in South Louisiana is given the pretty name, "Pomette Bleue." The low spreading tree is a mass of white flowers in spring, and in fall and winter is covered with clusters of blue fruit.

A charming tree in spring is Silverbell, *Halesia diptera.* Before the leaves are out, every twig is hung with white bells, grace itself. *Halesia carolina* has smaller flowers, but they are borne in profusion. Both of these occur in rich heavy soil along creek banks, but are easily transplanted and thrive in most any location. *Halesia diptera* is hardy to Philadelphia, and *H. carolina* to New England. The closely related Snowbell, *Styrax grandifolia,* is lovely, too, but the flowers open out like stars, instead of bell-shaped. They are borne in dainty sprays, and are very fragrant. There are several native species, but this is the best as it begins blooming when only two feet in height. I much prefer it to the Oriental *S. obassia,* for in the latter the large leaves tend to conceal the flowers. But *of course* this exotic is the only one offered in catalogs!

The delicious perfume of wild Crabapples should endear them to gardeners did they possess no other charms. But how often does one see them planted? The flowers of most species are delicate pink, and very fragrant. My favorite is *Malus angustifolia,* which begins blooming when only five or six feet tall. The flowers are not as large as those of *M. coronaria,* but are borne in

THREE NATIVE CRABAPPLES:
1. MALUS IOENSIS. 2. MALUS CORONARIA. 3. MALUS AUGUSTIFOLIA.

such profusion the branches "weep" with the weight of
blossoms. Alas, because of cedar-apple rust, native crabapples cannot be grown where there are Cedars, *Juniperus virginiana*. Give me the Malus and eliminate
the Juniperus!

Viburnums are represented by some charming trees
and shrubs in eastern and mid-western states, most of
them extremely hardy. Maple-leaved Viburnum, *V.
acerifolium*, is a pretty little under-shrub, with maple-
like leaves, small panicles of white flowers, and shining
black berries. Its most attractive feature is its unusual

color in late fall. After trees and big shrubs are bare, the leaves become pink and rose, forming a sheet of loveliness in the autumn woods. I have seen it stated that the leaves become purple. Well, all that I can say is, they are not "purple" in *my* woods! This one loves shade, and will grow in the poorest, dryest soil.

On the other hand, *Viburnum nudum* loves a bog and plenty of sun. The big ovate leaves are thick and shining, the panicles of cream-white flowers up to six inches across. The berries are beautiful, first whitish-green, then pink, then blue, with all three colors showing at the same time. It bears when not more than three feet high, but sometimes reaches six feet. It occurs in the wild to New York, and should be hardy almost anywhere. A species with similar beautiful fruits, *V. cassinoides*, is a tall slender shrub or small tree, with long pointed leaves. It is quite hardy. *Viburnum scabrellum* is a large shapely shrub, similar to *V. dentatum*. The panicles of cream-white flowers are six inches across, and the masses of stamens give them a soft look which is lovely. The berries are black, and in late fall the leaves take on rich shades of red. It is found to Pennsylvania, and is common in hardwood forests from Florida to Texas.

Two low trees, *Viburnum prunifolium* and *V. rufidulum*, are attractive when grown in the open where they can assume their natural rounded form. Both have shining ovate leaves and bear fairly large panicles of cream flowers. The drooping fruits are first rose-red, then bloomy-blue, the stems retaining their red color. The edible berries hold into early winter, and are very much relished by birds.

The beautiful High Cranberry Bush, *V. americanum*, is found in most of the northern states, and is often grown in gardens. The leaves are prettily lobed, the panicles of white flowers are edged with very white sterile ones (as in Hydrangeas), and the clustered fruits are bright red. Another species with sterile flowers ringing the big panicles of bloom, and red berries, is Hobble Bush, *V. alnifolium*. A big broad shrub, sometimes to ten feet, it is found in damp ground from Michigan to North Carolina. Alas, these two beauties cannot endure the hot summers of the Deep South, and I have never succeeded in growing either.

But there is one species which is a real southerner, *Viburnum obovatum*, and it is unique in that it is evergreen (except in extremely cold weather). Small gives it as occurring from Virginia to Florida, but I have seen it only on the Appalachicola River (Florida). It is most adaptable, and here it is growing in poor sandy soil. The leathery leaves are never more than one and a half inches long, and grow in clusters all along the stems, giving the plant a nice "leafy" look. The panicles of white flowers are not large, but are borne in profusion. The clusters of small fruits are first rose, then black. It begins to bloom when only a shrub, but eventually becomes a low graceful tree. Here at Briarwood it has not been harmed by zero weather, but does shed its leaves.

There are two large evergreen shrubs that seem to be almost unknown to horticulture, though very attractive. In sunny spots, *Cyrilla racemiflora* is a big shapely shrub, with long slender leaves, one of which, here and there, becomes bright red at any time of year. In late spring and early summer it is a mass of foamy white, the branching sprays with long fingers close-set with tiny flowers. In its native haunts it is found growing in damp ground, but is very adaptable and does well in the garden. The closely related Titi, *Cliftonia monophylla*, has much smaller leaves, and short unbranched racemes of tiny flowers, which may be either white or light pink. Cyrilla is found in the wild from Virginia to East Texas, and Cliftonia from Georgia to Florida and Mississippi. They often form solid hedges along roadsides near the Gulf Coast. Neither was damaged in the least by zero weather here at Briarwood. Both these big shrubs are most attractive, and deserve horticultural experimentation.

Yellow-wood, *Cladrastis lutea,* seems to be little known, although I have read that there is a specimen growing in Washington which attracts many visitors when in bloom. It is a small tree, with compound, light-green leaves, much like those of Ash. When hung with its drooping racemes—more than a foot long—of white-pea-shaped flowers it is a charming sight. It is reported as growing only in Tennessee, Kentucky, and North Carolina, but is very adaptable. Mine, planted in dry sandy soil, has survived many droughts—but I will have to admit it does not bloom! This is one native species that may be found in catalogs.

The *Fothergillas* are attractive shrubs, seldom seen in gardens. Three species are found in the Southeastern States, but *F. major* is the best. It is a shapely shrub, with rather rounded dentate leaves, and short spikes of white "bottle-brush" flowers. Edgar Anderson says they have had *F. monticola* for years at the Missouri Botanical garden. It grew very well for me in loose

FOTHERGILLA MAJOR, A BEAUTIFUL NATIVE
SHRUB WHICH DOES WELL IN THE GARDEN.

sandy soil, until it was crowded out by larger growing trees.

Huckleberries are attractive and useful plants, which range in size from dwarfs to big shrubs. *Vaccineum elliotti*, a twiggy graceful bush, is my favorite. The small pinkish flowers appear in very early spring, before the leaves. The small rounded leaves cling till early winter, when they become brilliant red. The little black berries are quite palatable. *V. frondosum* has much larger leaves, rather rough, but they, too, take on beautiful colors in autumn. The berries, borne in clusters, are blue. The Mountain Blueberry, *V. pallidum*, has a more restricted distribution, being found from Virginia to North Alabama. Even the botanists say the fruit is "delicious." The cultivated Blueberries, advertised in catalogs, were developed from native species, but for some reason they do not thrive for me, although wild Huckleberries grow all through my woods. *Vaccineum arboreum*, shrub or low tree, is most attractive, but I have never seen it in a catalog. In sunny spots, it assumes a spreading picturesque form, very twiggy. In spring it is a lacy mass of white, the short racemes of little urn-shaped flowers covering the plant. They look and smell like Lilies-of-the-valley, filling the air with perfume. The small rounded leaves glisten in the sun, and in late fall become rich red. The little black berries cling all winter, a feast for the birds. All Huckleberries must have acid soil, and like plenty of humus.

Sourwood, *Oxydendron arboreum*, is one of our most beautiful small trees. The pointed leaves are pretty at all times, but in early fall they cover the tree with glory, taking on shades from pink to crimson. As an extra

WINTER HUCKLEBERRY; VACCINIUM ARBOR-
EUM. A FAVORITE "DISH."

bonus, in June and July, they put out long branched racemes of fragrant white flowers. The little flowers are shaped like those of the Huckleberries, to which it is related. In Louisiana they become small trees before flowering, but on mountainsides in North Carolina and Alabama they bloom when only shrub-size, their delicate fragrant sprays gracing steep banks, hanging lovingly over roadsides. Sourwood must have acid soil, as it is related to the Huckleberries.

Pieris and *Leucothoe* belong in this same family, but as—with a few exceptions—they are evergreen, they will be described in that category. The first exception is *Leucothoe recurva*, a shrub with light-green pointed leaves, from the axils of which spring long, recurving, one-sided racemes of small white flowers. While not showy, they are singularly graceful, and fill the air with a delightful exotic fragrance. It is found in the wild from Virginia to Mississippi. *Pieris mariana* is a deciduous low shrub which, in early spring, is covered with short racemes of light-pink flowers, when it is quite attractive. It should be hardy, as it occurs as far north as Rhode Island. The most beautiful of the entire group is *Zenobia pulverulenta*, a graceful deciduous shrub, with whitish-green leaves. The big white flowers are borne in drooping racemes, and cover the plant before the leaves appear. Although it is offered by a few nurseries, it seems to be little known. It is found from North Carolina to Florida. Mine flourishes on a damp hillside, acid, sandy soil.

One of the most satisfactory of spring-blooming shrubs is Oakleaf Hydrangea, *H. quercifolia*. It is showy, easy to grow, and is attractive most of the year. The tall spires of flowers last for weeks, first white, then becoming rose. In fall, the leaves take on shades of deep rich red. I fell in love with it when I first saw it cascading down mountainsides in eastern states, but it is adaptable and will grow almost anywhere, except in alkaline soils. It will do very well in sun, but the flowers are whiter and prettier when planted in high shade. This is one native shrub which is now advertised in many catalogs.

Red Buckeye, *Aesculus pavia*, attracts much attention when bearing its bright-red spires of bloom in spring.

But before that, the unfolding leaf-buds are lovely in shades of flesh, pink, and rose. In fall, the big fruits open to disclose fat seeds in cream and brown, and these are used by flower arrangers. It is an accommodating shrub, for when cut to the ground, it puts up new shoots which bloom the same year. For this reason it could be treated as a perennial north of its natural range.

Lovely White Buckeye, *Aesculus parviflora*, is a more eastern species, occurring from South Carolina to Florida. It is a shapely shrub bearing cylindrical long spikes of small, close-set white flowers, very fragrant. The numerous long stamens give it a fluffy look, and it is sometimes called the Bottle-brush Buckeye. It is adaptable as to soil but wants good drainage and high shade. It is seldom found in catalogs. Yellow Buckeye, *Aesculus octandra*, is an attractive low tree, well known in eastern states. The spikes of flowers are usually light yellow.

Most gardeners grow the Asiatic Spiraeas, not knowing that we have some native species that are also well worthwhile. Meadow-sweet, *Spiraea alba*, is found from New York to Missouri and South to Georgia. It is a shrub to six feet, with loose panicles of small fragrant white flowers. Steeplebush, *S. tomentosa*, seems to be better known, and is offered by some nurserymen. It is a shrub, branching from the base, with loose graceful spires of small light pink flowers, and blooms all summer. It grows from Nova Scotia, south to Georgia, and west to Kansas. It is most adaptable, and does well here in Northwest Louisiana, in well drained and sandy soil. Western states also have native Spiraeas. *S. densiflora* is a low shrub with flowers in small corymbs, pink. *S. menziesii* is also pink, but flowers are borne in narrow panicles.

Oakleaf Hydrangea; H. quercifolia.
A beautiful shrub that is easy to
grow.

Almost everyone loves fragrant flowers, so no southern planting is complete without at least one clump of Sweet Shrub, *Calacanthus florida*. The brown-crimson flowers begin coming before the leaves appear, and fill the air with the delightful aroma of ripe strawberries. It is found in open woods, from Virginia to Florida and Louisiana, but can be grown a good deal farther north. It will thrive in almost any soil, if well drained. It spreads by stolons, so should not be planted too near smaller shrubs. A very similar species, *C. occidentalis*, is native to California, but is not hardy farther north.

On large grounds, where space does not have to be considered, common Elder, *Sambucus canadensis*, makes a fine showing. It grows naturally in big shapely clumps, six or seven feet high and as much broad, with enormous panicles of white flowers all the early summer. These are followed by shining black berries with red stems, and often both flowers and fruits are borne at the same time. And how birds do flock to this feast! It grows almost everywhere, from Canada to Florida to Arizona. A more northern species, *S. pubens*, bears red fruits, and may be found from North Georgia to northern parts of California. A similar species with beautiful red berries, *S. callicarpa*, is known as Pacific Red Elder, as it is native to the Pacific Coast Region. Some botanists consider it the same species as S. pubens. Blueberry Elder, *Sambucus glauca*, has a wide distribution in the West, from Canada to Southern California and extreme Southwest Texas. As the name suggests, the fruits are blue, and are used in making pies and jellies. All the Elders are adaptable as to soils, and easy to grow.

RED BUCKEYE; AESCULUS PAVIA; SHRUB.

To round out the year, our lovely native Witch Hazel hangs out its yellow fringy flowers in November and December, and perfumes all the woods. It begins to bloom when only a few feet high, but eventually becomes a big shrub. If topped and pruned back it produces many more flowers. This is *Hamamelis virginiana*, but the blooms on individual plants vary very much, some having much longer petals, ranging in color from cream to deep yellow. It is found growing in loose soil on hillsides. For some reason it is difficult to transplant, and is best grown from seed.

BEAUTIFUL BUT DIFFICULT

It must be stated that three beautiful native shrubs are temperamental. They can be grown with ease in their natural range, but seldom succeed outside of same. Perhaps they require some trace element. All three belong to the same family as Camellias, and one would expect them to grow where the latter thrive, but it does not work out this way. What is needed here is a real soil analysis, but that is difficult to obtain.

The famous "Lost Franklinia" is too well known to need description. It is a big shrub, in late summer bearing large white flowers with golden anthers. The serrate leaves are deciduous, which distinguishes it from the closely related *Gordonia lasianthus*, with which it is sometimes confused. The Bartrams discovered it in Georgia, named it *Franklinia alatamaha*, and established it in their garden near Philadelphia, or it would have been truly lost to horticulture. I fell in love with *Gordonia lasianthus* when I saw it growing around the clear shallow lakes and ponds in Central and Western Florida. As

The famous "Lost Franklinia."

they fell, entire, the cupped white flowers covered the ground. It refuses to grow for me, but thrives and flowers profusely for Sara Gladney at Baton Rouge (Louisiana) , and for Mrs. A. F. Storm near Charleston. Certainly beautiful *Stewartia malocodendron* should never be attempted outside its natural range, for it is not a garden plant. A large shrub, with flat lateral branches, in spring it bears its three-inch white flowers, with a ring of violet anthers in the center. It is one of our rarest shrubs, but there are a few groves in various parts of the South, and these should be rigidly protected and preserved.

Our lovely native Azaleas are not garden plants, but can be grown by those with the proper environment. They are very demanding, wanting loose acid soil and plenty of moisture, but perfect drainage. The first to bloom are two similar species, *A. nudiflora* and *A. canescens.* Both bear fluffy clusters of pink flowers before the leaves appear and form masses of exquisite bloom, very fragrant. At the same time, *A. austrina,* gives us similar flowers in various shades of yellow. Just a little later the dwarf *A. alabamense* is covered with clusters of big white flowers, each bearing one yellow spot. The delicious perfume is different from that of other azaleas. It can be grown on dryer ground than the preceding species, and forms sheets of bloom on mountainsides in its native Alabama.

Azalea viscosa is not as showy as the preceding species, but the white flowers are attractive when massed under tall trees, and it prolongs the season of bloom into early summer. The flowers are very sticky to the touch, and strong winds mar them. It is usually a low shrub, found growing in wet ground. This is sometimes confused with

AZALEA ARBORESCENS; LARGE SHRUB.

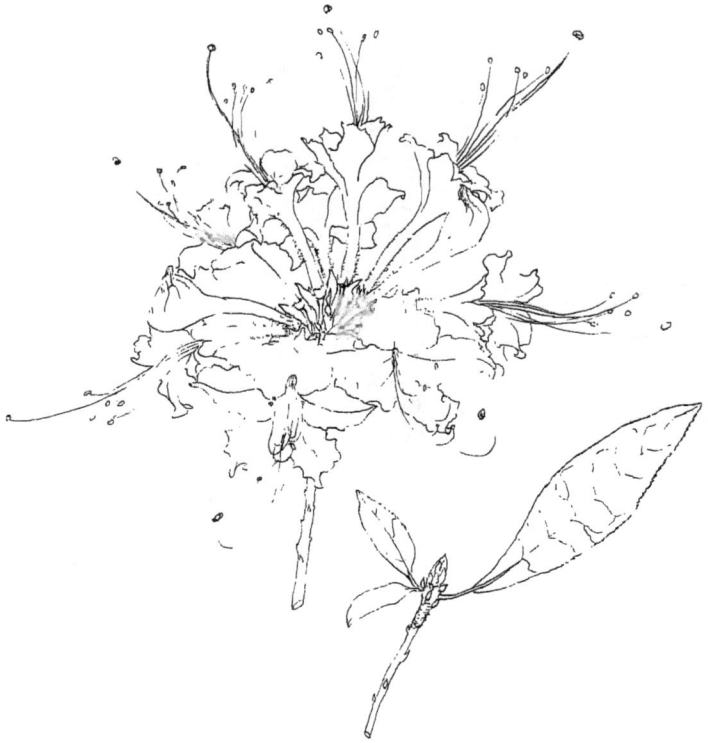

AZALEA   ALABAMENSE;   WHITE,   YELLOW   SPOT.

A. serrulata, but the latter is quite different, the only
similarity being that both bear white flowers. *A. serrulata* does not bloom until it becomes a large shrub or
small tree, and comes into flower in late July.

In the mountains in the eastern states *Azalea calendulacea* truly earns its common name, Flame Azalea, for
it is like fire creeping up the slopes. The clustered flow-

ers are wide open, in various shades of deep yellow and red, with one orange spot. They lack the sweet perfume of most native species. The plants are usually very low and spreading. It has been my observation that these spectacular flowers cannot be grown at low elevations. The most astonishing Azalea of all is *A. prunifolia*, with big flowers of an indescribable clear light red, and coming into flower in late July and early August, several months later than *A. calendulacea*. It occurs only in South-central Georgia and Alabama, but thrives here at Briarwood, on a sandy hillside, in high shade. In Georgia, I saw it growing under big Beech trees. I do not know what it may endure in the way of cold, but Mary G. Henry has a plant twelve feet across at Gladwyne (Pennsylvania)! In the proper environment native Azaleas make a wonderful display, as has been demonstrated at Callaway Gardens in Georgia, and Hodges Gardens in Louisiana, but they are not garden plants in the common sense. The Azalea Trail at Coleman's Nursery, Fort Gaines, Georgia, is beautiful and interesting.

All things considered, it seems to me that Mountain Laurel, *Kalmia latifolia*, is our finest native shrub. A shapely, beautiful plant, with its glossy evergreen leaves, it is well worth growing if it never bore a blossom. But in spring it is covered with the cupped flowers of luscious pink. It is not difficult to grow if given loose acid soil and good drainage. In the Deep South it prefers high shade. It is found from Florida and Louisiana to New England, and is quite hardy.

Most botanists put Rhododendrons and Azaleas in one genus, but as American Rhododendrons are evergreen and Azaleas deciduous, it is less confusing to many of us

RHODODENDRON MINUS. DWARF. SOFT PINK.

to keep them separate. The big Rhododendrons are
spectacular in their native mountains, but do not fit
into garden planting as does Mountain Laurel. On gray
rock bluffs above waterfalls, the trying magenta color of
R. maxima is no longer harsh but beautiful. Two species
native to the Alleghany Mountains are highly recommended as garden plants by Ernest Wilson. Both are

low compact shrubs which flower profusely, and both are hardy to New England. These are *R. carolinianum*, with pink to light purple flowers, and *R. catawbiense*, lilac-purple. These are not successful in the extreme South, except in mountainous regions. The only species that will grow in the Deep South is *R. minus*, a low shrub with small leaves and delicate pink flowers. It is a native of South-central Georgia and Alabama.

With very few exceptions, all species thus far described under flowering trees and shrubs are for eastern and mid-western states. However, *Cornus florida* and a few others do very well in Washington and Oregon.

FOR THE BLACK LANDS

This odd formation of heavy alkaline soil extends from Southwest Texas to North Dakota. Why should gardeners in this region struggle with eastern plants when they have so many beautiful species that are indigenous to the region? Who wants to see *Kalmia latifolia* in West Texas when they can revel in the beauty of "Texas Mountain Laurel," *Sophora secundiflora?* The latter is not even related to the eastern Mountain Laurel, but belongs to the legumes. It is a shapely evergreen shrub, with compound shining leaves, and racemes of lavender-blue flowers. Later, brown beans open to display glistening scarlet seeds, similar to those of Erythrina. This fine shrub can be grown in other localities where there is heavy rich soil, on the alkaline side. Blythe Rand has two magnificent specimens in her garden at Alexandria, on Red River in Louisiana.

An almost unknown but attractive low evergreen is Agarita, *Berberis trifoliata*, which is very different from most other Barberries. The prickly leathery leaves are much like those of Holly, except that they grow in threes. The tiny flowers, borne in tight clusters, are not showy, but possess a pervasive perfume. These are followed by sour bright red berries, which are used in jelly making.

The almost white leaves of *Leucophylla texanum* give it its botanical name. In South Texas it is called Ceniza. After every rain pinkish-lavender flowers appear in the axils of the leaves, when the shapely shrubs are a lovely sight. They are low and branching, with small rounded leaves, and are most attractive massed. By adding crushed lime rock, I grow them at Briarwood, but they do not flower as freely as in their native Texas. These last three shrubs cannot endure extreme cold, but to my surprise, Willie Mae Kell says that she grows them at Wichita Falls, Texas, where temperatures must drop pretty low.

Flowering Willow, *Chilopsis linearis*, is a small Texas tree which bears lovely lavender flowers, shaped like those of the Bignonias. Rarely a white one is found, and this is especially charming, as it noticeably displays the yellow spots in the throat. *Chilopsis* is deciduous, and inclined to become rather straggling if not pruned occasionally. Its native habitat is from Texas to Southern California, but Mrs. Cammie Henry grew it successfully at Melrose Plantation. This is on Cane River, Louisiana, where the soil is very fertile, and neutral. It probably will not survive temperatures as low as ten degrees.

The well-known Mesquite is an attractive low tree which might well be given a place on large grounds. The less known *Sophora affinis* is a slender deciduous tree, with pinnate leaves, and racemes of small lavender

pea-shaped flowers. Small* gives it as "growing on lime-
stone prairies, Arkansas and Texas." The late Lillian
Trichel had attractive specimens in her garden at Shreveport (Louisiana). Her soil was heavy rich clay, on the
alkaline side.

Salvia greggii is a charming small shrub found in
South Texas. It branches freely from the ground, has
tiny leaves, and bright-rose flowers. It is surprisingly
adaptable, and by adding crushed limerock, I grow it
here at Briarwood. If watered during droughts, it
blooms right through summer, until frost. Zero weather
got it, but as I had rooted cuttings I did not lose it. I
was very glad, for it is seldom seen in a catalog.

Spanish Bayonet, Yucca, thrives in the Southwest,
and by many is considered to typify the region. *Yucca
treculeana* is a native species, but several others of tree
size are grown. The form is always picturesque, and all
bear large trusses of cream-white bells. The Spaniards
called them by the lovely name, "Candles of the Lord."

THE WEST COAST STATES

The flowering trees and shrubs of California, alone,
would fill a volume, so necessarily only a few outstanding
species can be listed in this small book. John Muir's
description of the Madronas made me wildly envious of
California! Imagine a large, shapely, evergreen tree, with
reddish bark, panicles of white flowers, and bright red
fruits . . . this is *Arbutus menziesii*, a mountain species.
Arbutus arizonica is about half the size of the above, with
white trunk, red twigs, and pale green leaves. It, too,

---

* Flora of the Southeastern States, J. K. Small.

bears big loose panicles of white flowers, and red fruits. As its name indicates, this Madrona's range extends into Arizona.

California may claim the most glorious of dogwoods, *Cornus nuttallii*, a spreading tree which sometimes attains a height of eighty feet. The cream-white flowers are six inches across, followed by attractive red fruits. Unfortunately, this beautiful tree has not been a success outside the region to which it is native. Alfred Rehder describes *Fremontia californica* as "a beautiful free-flowering shrub . . . with large yellow flowers appearing in great profusion in June." It prefers a rather dry sunny slope. It is not hardy in the North.

A native of the Rocky Mountains, *Jamesia americana* is a handsome shrub with rather small leaves and panicles of white flowers. Occasionally a pink form is found. It is deciduous, but is attractive in the shrubby border. It thrives on sandy, well drained slopes, acid soil. It is said to be quite hardy.

Almost every state can claim some species of Elderberry, and the beautiful Pacific Red Elder grows in Washington, Oregon, and California. It is a big shapely shrub, bearing large panicles of red berries. This is *Sambucus callicarpa*, which means "beautiful fruit." Blueberry Elder, *S. glauca*, has a wider range, from California to Washington, and across to Southern New Mexico and Southeastern Arizona. It bears panicles of attractive blue berries, which are used in the making of pies and jellies.

But the glory of the Pacific slopes are the Wild Lilacs, so called because of their panicles of fragrant blue flowers, although they are not related to true Lilacs. One of the showiest is *Ceanothus thyrsiflorus*, a shrub or small tree, with panicles of flowers in beautiful shades of blue. It flowers profusely from May to July, and grows on sunny slopes from California to Oregon. *Ceanothus azureus* and *C. hirsutus* are also shrubs or small trees, with panicles of flowers in various shades of blue, rarely white. *C. spinosus*, with spiny leaves and panicles of light blue, grows on the Coast Range in California, down to sea level.

Because the Pacific Coast species belong to the same genus as our little *Ceanothus americanus*, found in the eastern states, I thought I could grow them at Briarwood, but to my sorrow they fade out in our hot dry summers. There are some attractive hybrids between *Ceanothus americana* and the blue-flowered California species, and these may prove to be more successful in the South.

Because of their adaptability, the remarkable group of shrubs belonging to the genus Mahonia deserve more attention. Most species are native to Oregon, and the common name is "Oregon Grape," because of the clusters of blue fruits. Surprisingly, *Mahonia aquifolium*, *M. pinnata*, *M. repens*, and a few others are hardy to New England, if shielded from winter winds. Even more amazingly, they flourish as far South as North Louisiana, if planted in cool semi-shaded locations. All have handsome evergreen foliage, panicles of bright-yellow flowers, and clusters of berries of an unusual shade of blue. The latter cling all winter.

IN VERY EARLY SPRING, SHADBLOW (AMA-
LANCHIER) HANGS OUT ITS DAINTY WHITE
FLOWERS. IT BECOMES A SMALL TREE,
BUT WILL BLOOM WHEN ONLY A SHRUB.

SUMMARY, FLOWERING TREES AND SHRUBS

(Zone numbers mean just one thing, that a plant will not be killed by cold in a given zone. For example, Zone 8 extends all the way from North Louisiana, up the West Coast to Oregon. But this by no means proves that Oregon species will succeed in Louisiana, for very few will.)

FOR THE EAST
(Some of these can be grown in the Mid-west, also)

Kalmia latifolia and Azaleas, zones 6 to 8, East. Acid soil, humus.

Rhododendrons (not including Azaleas), zones 5 to 8, East of Louisiana. Acid soil, coolness.

Pieris and *Leucothoe*, zones 5 to 8, East. Acid soil, moisture.

Zenobia pulverulenta, zones 7 to 9, East. Acid soil, moisture.

Sourwood, *Oxydendrum arboreum*, small tree, zones 5 to 8. Acid soil.

Cladrastis lutea, small tree, 5 to 8, East. Very adaptable.

Magnolia grandiflora, large evergreen tree, zones 7 to 9, parts of six.

M. macrophylla, zones 7 to 9, medium tree. In sites sheltered from winds. Shade while young.

Magnolia virginiana, 5 to 9. Medium tree. Acid soil.

M. acuminata, 5 to 8, east of Oklahoma. Large tree. Acid or neutral.

M. fraseri and *M. pyramidata*, 7 and 8, hills in 9. Small trees, acid. Can be grown east of Oklahoma.

STYRAX GRANDIFOLIA; SHRUB.

Tulip Tree, *Liriodendron tulipifera*, 5 to 8, to Oklahoma and East Texas. Acid.

Dogwood, *Cornus florida*, 5 to 9, to East Texas and E. Oklahoma. Small tree. Light acid soil, hills.

White Buckeye, *Aesculus parviflora*, 7 and 8. Shrub, high shade, rich soil.

Yellow Buckeye, *Aesculus octandra*, 5 to 8. Medium tree. Rich soil.

Red Buckeye, *Aesculus pavia*, 7 to 9, to East Texas.
Shrub. Hills, acid soil.

Fothergillas, several species, 5 to 8, east. Shrubs. Rich
soil, hills.

Hydrangea quercifolia, 7 to 9, east. Shrub. Light rich
soil, acid.

Sweet Shrub, *Calacanthus floridus*, 7 to 9 east. Shrub,
light rich soil, acid.

Silverbell, *Halesia diptera*, 6 to 9, small tree, rich light
soil, acid.

Halesia carolina, 7, to East Texas, and E. Oklahoma.
Small tree. Hills.

Cyrilla racemiflora, 8 to 9, to E. Texas. Small tree. Low
rich ground, acid.

Titi, *Cliftonia monophylla*, 8 to 9, east of Louisiana.
Small tree. Low ground. Acid.

Star anise, *Illicium floridanum*, 8 to 9, east. Shrub. Light
acid soil. Shade.

Spanish Dagger, *Yucca aloifolia*, and *Y. flaccidum*, 7 to 9
Southeast. Large shrubs. Prefer heavy soils, but very
adaptable.

Snowbell, *Styrax grandifolia*, *S. pulverulenta*, and *S.
americana*, 7, 8, and northern parts of 9, to E. Texas.
Large shrubs, usually near streams.

FOR THE WEST

Arbutus arizonica, 7 west. Tree, acid soil, well drained
site.

Jamesia americana, 5 and 6 west. Shrub, well drained
acid sandy soil.

Mesquite, *Prosopis*, several species, 6, 7, and 8 west. Low
trees, heavy soil, preferably alkaline.

FOR THE BLACKLANDS (ALKALINE), SOUTHWEST

Flowering Willow, *Chilopsis linearis*, large shrub. 8, rich heavy soil.

Texas Mountain Laurel, *Sophora secundiflora*, 8 and 9, alkaline or neutral.

Sophora affinis, small tree, heavy rich soil, alkaline or neutral.

Leucophylla texana, 8, shrub. Grown in various sites, lime added if soil acid.

Agarita, *Berberis trifoliatum*, 8, shrub. Will grow in sand if lime added.

Salvia greggii, shrub. 8. Will grow in sandy soil if lime is added.

ARID REGIONS OF THE WEST, zones 5, 6, and 7, to WEST TEXAS

In this area, other trees and shrubs are largely replaced by various species of Cactus, too numerous to be described in this volume. Saguero, Ocotillo, and the Chollas attain tree size, and are spectacular in the landscape. There are Cacti in all sizes, and all bear beautiful flowers. Attractive gardens in this area are created of Cacti, alone. However, plantings can be varied by adding Agave, Palo Verde, and some species of Yucca.

MAY BE GROWN PRACTICALLY EVERYWHERE, EXCEPT IN ARID AREAS

Wild Crabapples, *Malus*, many species. Low trees. Various soils.

RARELY SEEN IN CULTIVATION, ZENOBIA
PULVERULENTA IS ONE OF THE FINEST
SHRUBS OF THE LARGE HEATH FAMILY.
THE LOVELY WHITE BELLS ARE MOST
GRACEFUL.

Shadblows, *Amalanchier,* many species. Low trees. Various soils.

Hawthorns, *Crataegus,* many species. Low trees. Various soils.

Wild Plums, *Prunus,* many species. Low trees. Various soils.

Viburnums, many species, mostly eastern. Various sites.

Elders, *Sambucus,* several species. Big shrubs. Usually
  acid soils.
Steeplebush, *Spiraea tomentosa.* Shrub. Well drained
  sites.
Witch Hazel, *Hamamelis.* Big shrub. Light acid soil.
Huckleberries, *Vaccinium,* various species. Shrubs. Acid
  soils.

MAGNOLIA GRANDIFLORA.
Photograph by Elemore Morgan.

EVERGREENS

In choosing evergreens, tastes differ so radically it is difficult to make recommendations. The following suggestions may be considered and acted upon according to individual preferences.

For large estates, the stately pines are magnificent, but it is a mistake to try to crowd them into small plots. In the hilly part of Shreveport (Louisiana), houses of classical beauty have been built in the midst of existing pine groves, and the effect is charming. Nothing is more beautiful than Longleaf Pine, *Pinus palustris*, with its clean red-brown trunks, and terminal tufts of fifteen-inch-long needles. The leaves glisten in sunlight, and the young trees are fountain-like in their grace. Eventually they reach a height of a hundred feet. Slash Pine is a similar species, but needles grow all along the stem. It is desirable as it grows very rapidly. It is a native of the Gulf coast, but is being successfully grown in many localities. Old-field Pine, *Pinus taeda*, is another rapid grower, with shorter needles, forming masses of deep green foliage. These Pines are most attractive when planted in groves, allowing the fallen needles to form a lovely brown carpet—so much prettier than grass! These are southern species, but can be grown much farther north than their native habitat. Spruce Pine, *Pinus glabra*, is a southern species which seems to be little known. This is not to be confused with the Spruce of the eastern states. The needles are very short, soft, and glistening, and the bark is almost smooth. The shapely young "Christmas trees" are beautiful when seen against white sand-banks of streams in the Southeast.

In the North, White Pine, *Pinus strobus*, is the tree for large grounds. B. E. Fernow (Bailey's Encyclopedia) says, "for grace and elegance nothing better can be suggested." This magnificent tree grows in most of the northern states, and South to the mountains of North Carolina and North Georgia. For western mountainous regions, Silver Pine, *Pinus monticola*, seems to be king, and according to John Muir,* it rules in "silvery splendour." He loved storms, and said pines were "the best interpreters of the winds."

An interesting small species is Pinon Pine, *Pinus edulis*. It begins bearing cones when very small, and these open and spill the delicious fat seeds, giving the tree another name, Nut Pine. The Indians of the region gather them in quantities and feast upon them. This little species grows in the mountains, on the dryest rocky slopes, from Wyoming to West Texas. I do not know whether or not it has been grown successfully in the East.

The Firs are noble trees, full of grace. Balsam Fir grows in most northern states, from Minnesota to New England, and south to Northern Pennsylvania. *Abies fraseri* is a more southern species, found in the Appalachian Mountains. White Fir, *Abies concolor*, is a beautiful species of the Northwest, with blue-green foliage. And on the West Coast is found *Abies amabilis*, admiringly called Lovely Fir, or Silver Fir. These fine trees are grown in their natural range, but it is possible this could be extended.

Spruces seem to be quite adaptable, and are often grown for their beauty. Colorado Blue Spruce, *Picea pungens*, is known for its attractive silvery foliage. It is

---

* The Wilderness World of John Muir, by Edwin Way Teale.

CANADA HEMLOCK; TSUGA CANADENSIS.

a native of the Rocky Mountain Region, but I saw a fine specimen on a lawn in Highland Park, Illinois. Black Spruce, *Picea mariana,* is a fairly small species, bearing its tiny purple cones when only a few feet tall. It is found from Canada to Virginia and to Minnesota, which gives it a fairly wide range. *Picea canadensis* is a much larger tree, with light blue-green foliage and little glossy-brown cones. It is a northern species, growing from Canada south to Montana and across to New York, but is said to withstand heat and drought better than most Spruces.

I shall never forget the first time I saw Canada Hemlock, *Tsuga canadensis*. It was growing on a ledge on the side of a rocky gorge in the mountains, and I could look down on its lovely pendulous branches. But the top was all around me where I stood, and I could touch it. It was October, and each ferny twig was tipped with a tiny cone. It can surely be grown in its wide natural range, from Wisconsin to Delaware, and South to Northeast Alabama. A smaller species, Carolina Hemlock, *Tsuga caroliniana*, is just as beautiful as the preceding. It is more Southern in its distribution, occurring in the Appalachian Mountains, from Virginia to Northern Georgia.

Canada Yew, *Taxus canadensis*, is quite different from other members of this big family. It is a rather sprawling, prostrate shrub, with shining light-green leaves, but fits nicely into certain spots, such as tops of steep banks. In cultivation it is a little more upright in habit. It is found from Canada to Virginia and across to Iowa, and is offered by some nurseries.

Red Cedar, *Juniperus virginiana*, is a graceful tree, but, alas, it bears brown balls which act as host to the disfiguring apple rust. So one must choose, Cedars or Crabapples. Oddly enough, our lovely native Crabs are more subject to this rust than the Asiatic species.

CAROLINA HEMLOCK; TSUGA CAROLINIANA.

Arbor Vitaes are quite popular, but they are too compact, too formal for my taste. A native species, *Thuga
occidentalis,* is found from Canada to North Carolina,
and is very adaptable.

In the Deep South, broadleaf evergreens are preferable to conifers—excepting the Pines—and seem more
fitting in the landscape. Why try to coax homesick
Spruces and Firs to grow, when one can have glorious
Magnolia grandiflora? And what could be finer than
a good specimen of American Holly, *Ilex opaca*, with its
pretty leaves and red berries? Unfortunately, Hollies
bear staminate and pistillate flowers on separate trees so
all do not bear fruit. However, nurseries offer grafted
plants, and insure berries. Yaupon, *Ilex vomitoria*, is a
smaller member of the Holly Family, with tiny glistening leaves and masses of red berries. It makes a fine
specimen, and is very attractive as an informal hedge.
It received its repellant botanical name from the fact that
Southern Indians prepared their famous "black drink"
from an infusion of the leaves. A coastal species, Dahoon,
Ilex cassine, is taller, with longer leaves, and clusters of
red berries.

Spacious grounds in the Deep South must boast at
least one Live Oak, *Quercus virginiana*. With its long
branches it often covers an area a hundred feet across,
and with its shining green leaves presents a beautiful picture. Visitors to Charleston, Savannah, and South Louisiana are familiar with the magnificent avenues of these
trees, hung with picturesque streamers of gray Spanish
Moss. Contrary to common belief, Live Oaks grow rapidly when planted in rich soil, where the water-table is
high.

In the sand hills, Live Oak is largely replaced by
Laurel Oak, *Quercus laurifolia*, another attractive species. The rather long narrow leaves are shining green,
with a white midrib on the reverse. This easily distin-

guishes it from Willow Oak and Water Oak, both deciduous. It is evergreen, but the leaves do not hold two
years, like those of Live Oak. They are pushed off in
spring by the new leaves. It is of more upright habit
than Live Oak, grows more rapidly, and in a short time
becomes a fine shade-tree. It is very easy to transplant
from the wild, and is widely used as a street tree in the
South. It occurs in the wild from New Jersey to Central
Florida, Louisiana, and E. Texas.

The well known Wax Myrtle, *Myrica cerifera* from
New Jersey to Florida and Texas, *M. pennsylvanica* from
New York to North Carolina, is an attractive and accommodating shrub. It is evergreen, with thick growth, and
can be kept low or allowed to become a round-topped
small tree. It usually occurs in coastal regions, but has
been found as far inland as Ohio. It assumes its finest
form along tidal waterways, where its green rounded
masses are most attractive. Both species are adaptable,
easy to grow, and are used to some extent in landscaping,
but deserve wider recognition.

The berries of both species of Wax Myrtle have a waxy
covering, hence the name. In pioneer days, berries were
gathered in quantity for the making of spicy Bayberry
candles. In the North it is better known as Bayberry,
but is sometimes called Wax-berry.

Wild Sweet Olive, *Osmanthus americana*, is an attractive evergreen which seems to be unknown in trade. It
is a small tree with rather large leathery leaves, and
axillary clusters of fragrant cream flowers. The perfume
is not as sweet as that of Osmanthus of gardens. It begins
blooming when a large shrub, but will eventually attain
a height of thirty feet. The large black fruits are rather

ornamental. It is found near streams, but will grow almost anywhere if given acid soil and humus. It occurs it the wild from Virginia to Florida to Southeastern Louisiana.

Titi, *Cliftonia monophylla*, is a pretty evergreen of coastal regions, from South Carolina to Florida and Mississippi. With its numerous small shining leaves, it is attractive as a single specimen or as a high hedge. As it also bears dainty pink or white flowers, it has been more fully described under Flowering Trees and Shrubs.

Another attractive southern evergreen is Star Anise, *Illicium floridanum*, a large shrub found from Northwestern Florida to Southeastern Louisiana. It has withstood zero temperatures here at Briarwood. The leathery leaves have a delightful aroma when bruised. It wants high shade, acid soil, and humus. It has showy red flowers, and is described in that chapter. Nurseries do not carry this beautiful shrub, but offer us *Illicium anisatum*, with its inconspicuous greenish-yellow flowers.

Rhododendrons and *Kalmia latifolia* are valuable as evergreens, even if they did not bear their beautiful flowers. The shapely Mountain Laurel is fine anywhere, but is especially effective on slopes, between big boulders, as it grows in its native habitat. It is hardy to New England, but this accommodating beauty will also withstand the excessive heat of the Deep South, if given plenty of humus and good drainage.

Pieris lucida (Lyonia nitida) belongs to the same big Heath Family, and is a charming low evergreen. The shining leaves are small, and the many branches arch most gracefully. It is lovely in the large rock garden, or in the front of the shrub border. *Leucothoe axillaris* is a somewhat similar plant, with large, thicker leaves, and numerous turned-down racemes of small white flowers in the axils of the leaves. It is low and spreading, and splendid for covering a bare spot. Beautiful *Leucothoe catesbaei* is better known, as it is much used by florists in wreaths and bouquets. The long, pointed leaves are thick and stiff, and take on red-bronzy tints in cold weather. In spring the long arching sprays bear numerous recurving racemes of tiny creamy urns. The buds are pretty all winter. Its natural range is from Virginia to Georgia, but mine is very happy here, on a shady hillside. Like all the family, it must have acid soil and humus. This one is sold by several nurseries. Quite different from the three preceding species in its manner of growth is *Pieris floribunda*, an upright shrub to six feet, thickly set with its leathery leaves, and masses of small white flowers in short racemes. It is a mountain species from Virginia to Georgia, but is offered by nurseries.

The Black Lands of the Southwest can claim two beautiful shrubby evergreens, Agarita, *Berberis trifoliata*, and "Texas Mountain Laurel," *Sophora secundiflora*, both of which are described under flowering species.

In California, Holly is replaced by lovely Toyon, *Photinia arbutifolia*, also called Christmasberry. A shrub or small tree, it has shining, sharply serrate leaves, and bright red berries all winter.

SUMMARY, EVERGREENS

(Zone numbers mean just one thing, that a plant will not be killed by cold in a given zone:)

Longleaf Pine, *Pinus palustris,* 7, 8, and N. part of 9. Lofty tree. Acid well drained soil.

Slash Pine, *P. caribaea,* 8 and 9, rapid growing tree, very adaptable.

Loblolly Pine, *P. taeda,* 7 and 8 to E. Tex. Large tree, very adaptable.

Spruce Pine, *P. glabra,* 8 and 9 east. Medium tree, sandy soil.

White Pine, *P. strobus,* 4 to N. part of 7. Mts. in south. Large tree.

Western White Pine, Silver Pine, *Pinus monticola,* 5 to 7 in mountains. Large tree.

Pinyon Pine, *P. edulis,* mountains in 5 and 6. Small tree, large edible seeds.

Balsam Fir, *Abies balsamea,* 4 and 5, east of Nebraska. Large tree.

Abies fraseri, 7 in Appalachian Mts. Short lived in cultivation.

Lovely Fir, *A. amabilis,* 8, in high mountains, only.

Silver Fir, *A. concolor,* 5, in mountains west. Very tall tree. Most satisfactory Fir in the eastern U. S.

Colorado Blue Spruce, *Picea pungens,* 5 to 7, Rocky Mts. to East Arizona. Adaptable. Large handsome tree.

Black Spruce, *P. mariana,* 3 to 5, east. Medium tree, varied forms.

White Spruce, *P. canadensis,* 4 and 5, east of S. Dakota. Handsome medium-sized tree, adaptable in cultivation.

Canada Hemlock, *Tsuga canadensis,* 5 to 7 east. S. to
   mts. of Ala. Beautiful large tree for cool situations.
Carolina Hemlock, *Tsuga caroliniana,* 7, Appalachian
   Mts. to N. Ga. Charming medium-sized tree, cool
   situations, usually acid soil.
Canada Yew, *Taxus canadensis,* 4 to 7. Prostrate large
   shrub.
Red Cedar, *Juniperus virginiana,* 4 to 8. Medium tree.
   Well drained site.
Arbor vitae, *Thuja occidentalis,* 4 to 7, east of Nebraska.
Magnolia grandiflora, 7, 8, and parts of 9, east. Very
   handsome, adaptable tree.
American Holly, *Ilex opaca,* 5 to 9, east. Beautiful med-
   ium-sized tree.
Yaupon, *Ilex vomitoria,* 7, 8, and 9, east of Cent. Tex.
   Shrub.
Dahoon, *Ilex cassine,* 7, 8, and 9, Coastal Plain, to S. E.
   La. Shrub.
Live Oak, *Quercus virginiana,* 7 to 9, Coastal Plain, to E.
   Tex. Big tree.
Laurel Oak, *Q. laurifolia,* 7 to 9, to E. Tex. Large quick
   growing tree.
Wax Myrtle, *Myrica cerifera,* 7 to 9, west to E. Tex. and
   SE. Oklahoma. Shrub.
Northern Wax Myrtle, Bayberry, 5 to 7, east of Illinois.
   Shrub.
Wild Sweet Olive, *Osmanthus americanum,* 7, 8, and
   northern parts of 9 to SE. La. Slender tree.
Titi, *Cliftonia monophylla,* 8 and 9, east of La. Small
   tree. Low ground.
Star Anise, *Illicium floridana,* 8 and 9, east of Tex. Large
   shrub. Shade.

Rhododendron maxima, 5 to 7, to N. Ala. mts. Big shrub, acid soil.

Rhododendron carolinianum, 5 to 7, mts. of Tenn. and N. C. Compact shrub.

Rhododendron catawbiense, 5 to 7, east, to mts. of N. Ga. Beautiful shrub.

Pieris floribunda, 5 to 7, Allegheny Mts. in N. Ga. Shrub, Acid soil.

Pieris lucida, 7, 8, and N. parts of 9, east. Low shrub. Acid, moist soil.

Leucothoe axillaris, 7, 8, and N. parts of 9, east. Low shrub. Acid soil.

Leucothoe catesbaei, 7, east. Beautiful shrub, shade, acid soil.

Berberis trifoliata, 8, alkaline soil, in sandy land if lime added. Shrub.

Sophora secundiflora, 8 and 9, Texas. Heavy soil, alkaline or neu. Shrub.

Toyon, *Photinia glabra,* California. Shrub or small tree.

VINES

This chapter will contain as many warnings as recommendations, for some species, though beautiful, can
become a curse. These require watchful care, and in a
large woodland, this is difficult and expensive. The
many birds here at Briarwood scatter seeds here and yon,
and young plants are constantly springing up.

Yellow Jessamine is a dainty vine, with small evergreen
leaves, slender brown stems, and masses of trumpet-
shaped bright yellow flowers. It begins blooming in
very early spring, and lasts for weeks. Here it festoons
every bush and tree, and the delicious perfume fills the
air. It is something of a spreader, but as it does not
strangle trees is not obnoxious. If it carpets the ground
no one would object. This is *Gelsemium sempervirens*,
not a "Jasmine" at all, as it is sometimes called. It occurs
in the wild from Virginia to Florida and Texas, but no
doubt can be grown much farther north.

There is a native Wistaria, *W. frutescens*, with racemes
of lavender flowers, shorter than those of Asiatic origin,
which is quite attractive. But, alas, Wistarias are the Boa
constrictors of the plant world, and must be watched,
else they will strangle and kill trees. They spread by
long root-runners and require constant care. Nothing
is more beautiful than Wistarias in bloom, and many
feel that they are well worth any amount of trouble.

Another importation from the Orient is *Lonicera
japonica*, often called Hall's Honeysuckle, but it has
"gone wild" in many places in this country. An attractive evergreen, with sprays of fragrant white flowers, it
became quite popular, especially as a ground-cover, and

107

was widely planted. It spreads rapidly, and birds eat the
berries and scatter the seeds far and wide. It is taking
over my beautiful woodland, smothering shrubs and
small trees. Nothing is finer for covering steep banks
along roadsides, but if there are farms nearby the owners
will object. In fact, I have read that the planting of
this pretty vine is forbidden in some states.

A related species, *Lonicera sempervirens*, commonly
called Woodbine, does not spread so rapidly and is not
such a menace. The glaucous-green leaves are attractive,
and the one on the flowering stem is perfoliate. The
clustered "honeysuckle" flowers are bright red—and how
hummingbirds love them! In the wild it rambles over
shrubs and low trees and is very pretty trained on an
arbor or fence.

Crossvine, *Bignonia capreolata*, is a high climber which
clings by tiny "feet," so does not strangle. The ovate
leaves are borne in pairs, and so are the rich-colored
flowers of typical Bignonia form. The latter are red on
the outside, warm yellow within, and the long sprays of
bloom swinging high in trees form a striking display.
Alas, this is one that bears watching, for it spreads rapidly
by long runners on the ground. This vine may not be
hardy very far north, as it occurs in the wild from Illinois
to Florida and Louisiana. The related Trumpet Vine,
Bignonia radicans, is a more showy species, with pinnate
leaves and clusters of bright-red "trumpets." The flowers make a gay display topping fence-posts along roadsides. . It is also attractive on walls and trellises. It thrives
in rich soil, from Missouri to Florida and Texas.

Beware of Rattan, *Berchemia scandens*, for it belongs
to the "Boa constrictor" vines! It is a high-climber, with

small leaves which turn lemon-yellow in late fall. The black berries are much appreciated by birds, for they cling till late winter.

Suddenly in autumn woods, a flame seems to be running up the trunks of trees, startlingly beautiful. This is Virginia Creeper, with the impossible botanical name, *Parthenocissus quinquefolia,* by some classed as *Ampelopsis.* It is found in woodlands from Canada to Florida, and west to Texas and Illinois. Its clinging habit makes it desirable for covering walls. Alas, its autumn fire is soon extinguished, for the leaves fall quickly. This is another species which runs over the ground, taking root as it goes, so must be watched to avoid undue spreading.

While condemning vines that travel, I will have to include that old favorite, Bittersweet, *Celastrus scandens.* It is a dainty vine, and in fall nothing is lovelier than its graceful sprays of red fruits. As almost everyone knows, these retain their color for months when cut. My experience with it was a sad one. When I bought it, I was so unfortunate as to get a male plant (staminate and pistillate flowers are borne on separate vines), so of course never had any fruit. But it spreads, and I am still digging it out.

It is surprising that no one seems to grow our native grapes on large grounds. There are many species, some high-climbing, some low, and all attractive. When clusters of fruit hang among the pretty leaves the effect is beautiful. There are too many species to be listed here, but they were so plentiful the Norsemen called North America Vineland! All bear edible fruit, some of which are delicious.

The popularity of modern Roses has overshadowed our lovely native species. At Cypress Gardens near

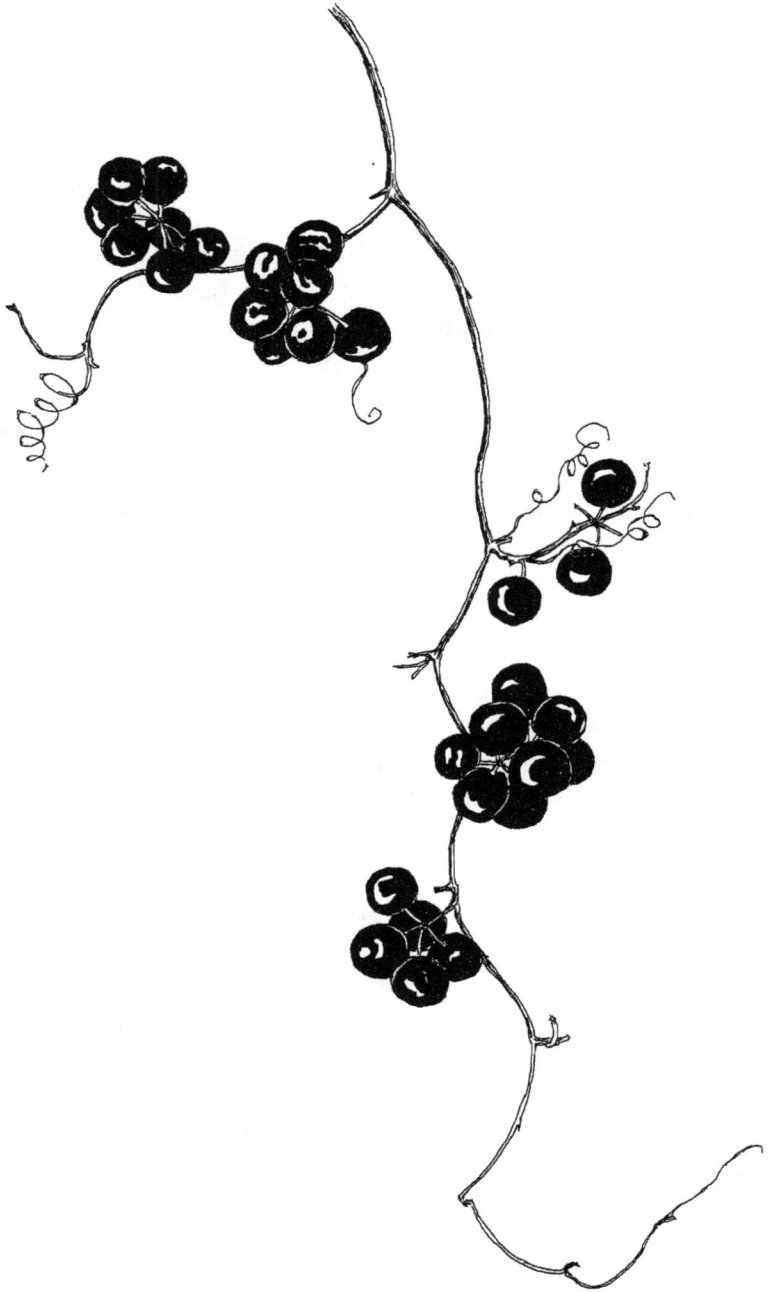

SMILAX WALTERI. (BRIGHT RED).

Charleston, I saw Cherokee Rose, *Rosa laevigata*, climbing the Cypress trees, with long streamers of big white flowers. These, with Yellow Jessamine and Wistaria, all reflected in the black water, formed an unforgettable picture. This rose is said to have come from China, but this is difficult to believe, for as long ago as Nuttall's day it was so widespread he thought it native. The glistening evergreen leaves are beautiful all winter, making it most attractive for hedges and arbors. When tied up to a post, it arches back most gracefully, a fountain of white when in bloom. It is unfortunate that it is so often confused with the McCartney Rose, *R. bracteata*, which is not as pretty, and which spreads so badly as to become a nuisance. About the only good thing to be said for it is that it was one parent of the exquisite pale-yellow Mermaid!

Prairie Rose, *R. setigera*, has the purest pink flowers of almost any species, and as these are borne in big loose clusters it is very showy. It is most accommodating, for it will climb to ten feet or more, or can be kept cut back to bush form. This species is quite hardy, and is now being used in crosses to produce a tough strain of garden varieties.

Some of our most charming native vines belong to the genus *Smilax*, but they, too, should be planted only on large grounds, as they spread. Graceful evergreen Southern Smilax, *S. lanceolata*, is beautiful on deciduous trees in winter, and it does not spread except where birds plant the berries. There are several evergreen species, but this is the prettiest. *Smilax walteri* is deciduous, and when one winter day I saw it scrambling over Button-bushes, I gasped. The clusters of fat bright-red berries simply covered the plant, very beautiful. I hate to keep telling bad news, but this is another "spreader," sending out stolons from the root. It loves the wet acid soil by the pond, so I just revel in its beauty—and *try* to keep it in bounds.

Another vine with long racemes of translucent red berries is *Cocculus carolinianum*. It belongs to the Moonseeds, for the seeds are in the form of tiny crescents. It is a slender vine, and lovely on trellises, but it, too, spreads by root-runners and has to be watched. It is native from Virginia to Florida, to Texas and Kansas.

Some of the perennial vines are charming, and none more so than the several native species of *Clematis*. Covering shrubs in damp ground, *C. virginiana* is very graceful. The clustered flowers are almost identical with those of the cultivated *C. paniculata*, except they are not as snowy-white. But when the clusters of feathery seed-plumes appear it exceeds the latter in beauty. A much smaller plant is dainty *Clematis crispa*, with prettily divided leaves, and urn-shaped blue flowers. *Clematis texana (coccinea)* is a similar vine, but the little urns are scarlet, making it the finest of the lot. Mine climbs over a twiggy Winter Huckleberry, where the bright-red flowers swing entrancingly. It occurs in Texas, only, and I cannot vouch for its hardiness, except to say that zero weather left it untouched. For some reason, this little gem is hard to find. Mine came from Ramsey Nursery, Austin.

Wild Potato, *Ipomoea pandurata*, has already been recommended as a ground-cover for steep banks, but it is also lovely as a low twining vine, with its big dark-centered white flowers. Its close relative, *I. macrorhiza*, is a heavier vine, bearing big lavender flowers of a lovely crepe texture, and prettily lobed leaves. It is a vigorous climber and quickly covers a trellis or low tree. It has a tremendous tuberous root, and probably was eaten by the Indians. Dr. Small called it Midden Morning-glory, because he found it on shell mounds in Florida. However, it should be Evening-glory, for the exquisite flowers open in late afternoon, closing the next morning. In very cloudy weather, they remain open most of the day.

The pretty Peas, *Bradburya*, lavender, and *Strophostyles*, pink, have been described as ground-covers, but they are also attractive little climbers. In a wild garden, they run up shrubs and grasses, displaying their colorful flowers for months. Both are perennials.

Maypop, *Passiflora incarnata*, is a charming vine that deserves more attention. The lobed leaves are pretty, and the lavender three-inch flowers are famous for their beauty and odd form. The large fruits are fragrant and edible. It is attractive as a ground-cover, but will climb any support provided for it. I do not know how far north it can be grown, but it occurs in the wild from Missouri to Florida and Texas. Almost unknown is a close relative, *Passiflora lutea*, a dainty vine with blunt-lobed leaves. The light-yellow flowers are only one inch across, but show the perfect Passion-flower form. The little fruits are black.

SUMMARY, VINES

Yellow Jessamine, *Gelsemium sempervirens,* 7 & 8, e. of
   Cen. Tex. Sandy acid soil.

American Wistaria, *W. frutescens,* 7 & 8, e. of Okla.
   Adaptable.

Lonicera sempervirens, 5 to 9 w. of Colo. Adaptable.
   Beautiful.

Hall's Honeysuckle, *L. japonica,* everywhere, escaped
   from cultivation. Pest.

Crossvine, *Bignonia capreolata,* 6 to 9, all zones except
   arid regions.

Trumpetvine, *C. radicans,* 7 to 9, e. of Cen. Tex. Adaptable.

Rattan, *Berchemia scandens,* 7 to 9, adaptable. Chokes
   out trees and shrubs.

Virginia Creeper, *Parthenocissus quinquefolia,* 3 to 9,
   e. of W. Tex.

Bittersweet, *Celastrus scandens,* 3 to 8 e. of Colo. Pretty,
   but spreads.

Wild Grapes, *Vitis.* Some species in almost every zone.

Cherokee Rose, *R. laevigata,* 7 to 9, very adaptable.

Macartney Rose, 8, 9. Spreads and becomes a nuisance.

Prairie Rose, *Rosa setigera.* Very hardy and adaptable.

Sou. Smilax, *S. lanceolata,* 7 to 9 e. of N. Mex. Dry soil.
   Attractive.

Sou. Smilax, *S. laurifolia,* 7 to 9, e. of N. Mex. Damp
   ground.

Red-berried Smilax, *S. walteri,* 7 to 9, e. of Miss. River.
   Damp Ground.

Red Moonseed, *Cocculus carolinianum,* 7 to 9, e. of W.
   Tex. Pretty. Spreads.

RED CLEMATIS; CLEMATIS TEXANA (FORMERLY
C. COCCINEA). A DAINTY PERENNIAL VINE.

Clematis virginiana, 4 to 9 e. of Colo. Adaptable.

Clematis crispa, 7 to 9, e. of W. Tex. Dry soil.

Clematis texana (coccinea), Tex. and La., probably other
sts. Dry sites.

Wild Potato, *Ipomoea pandurata*, 4 to 9 w. of N. Mex.
Dry sandy soil.

Ipomoea macrorhyza, 8 and 9, e. of Cen. Tex. Very
adaptable.

Butterfly Pea, *Bradburya virginiana*, 7 to 9, e. of N. Mex.
Dry soil.

Pink Partridge Pea, *Strophostyles umbellata*, 5 to 9, e.
of Kans. Sandy soil.

Maypop, *Passiflora incarnata*, 7 to 9. Dry sandy land.
Sun.

Dwarf Passionflower, *P. lutea*, 5 to 9. Dry acid soil.

PINK PARTRIDGE PEA

(STROPHOSTYLES UMBELLATA) COVERS THE GROUND, AND BEARS ITS PRETTY
FLOWERS ALL SUMMER. A PERENNIAL, IT WANTS LOOSE ACID SOIL, AND FULL SUN.

GROUND-COVERS

Ground-covers are almost a necessity, whether in the wild garden or in one devoted to cultivated species. They serve two important purposes: they hide bald unsightly spots, and help keep down weeds. There are many types, beginning with little Turkeyberry, *Mitchella repens*, which really hugs the ground. The tiny rounded leaves are evergreen, the starry velvety flowers perfume the air in May, and all winter the bright red berries cling—or until eaten by Robins. Twinberry is another fitting name for this pretty plant, for it takes two flowers (with united ovary) to form one berry. In the South it must have high shade to flourish, with acid soil and decaying leaves.

Dichondra is a dainty evergreen creeper, said to have been brought in from Europe, but if so, it has certainly "gone wild" in eastern states. It is spreading even here at Briarwood, and I cannot imagine how it could have been brought here. *Vinca minor*, too, is said to be a native of Europe, but is found in the wild from Canada to Georgia. It is an attractive trailing plant, with small evergreen leaves and occasional light-blue flowers. It is a desirable ground-cover, as it will grow in dense shade and dry soil, where few plants survive.

It seems to be little known that our lovely Yellow Jessamine, *Gelsemium sempervirens*, can be used as a ground-cover, especially on steep banks. I learned this by observing it where it was kept cut back by highway crews. The small pointed leaves are green in winter, and in spring it becomes a cascade of fragrant bright-yellow trumpets. Its natural range is from Virginia to Florida and Texas, but probably can be grown farther north.

117

When cut back by severe cold, it springs again from the root.

Fortunate gardeners in sandy lands from New Jersey to North Carolina can grow Sand Myrtle, *Leiophyllum buxifolium*. A low spreading evergreen, it has small box-like leaves—as the name indicates—and clusters of little starry white flowers. It is very attractive in the rock garden, or as a ground-cover on sandy slopes. It is found in the wild from New Jersey to North Carolina, and can be grown farther south in mountainous regions. It did not survive the heat here in Louisiana.

If I lived in California or Washington, I would plant my slopes with the prostrate Wild Lilac, *Ceanothus prostratus*. When this low evergreen covers itself with clusters of fragrant blue flowers, who could ask for more? Another low species is found from South Dakota to Arizona, and Alfred Rehder* calls it "a very graceful and free-flowering shrub of almost creeping habit, well adapted for covering dry sandy banks." The flowers of this species, *C. fendleri*, are white.

Some dealers in native plants recommend Trailing Arbutus as a ground cover, but it is demanding in its requirements and must be tried with caution. It should be purchased from a nursery, pot-grown, and planted in sandy, peaty soil, in a cool site. The practice of tearing it from its native environment for planting in gardens is hastening the end of this charming flower.

The two dwarf roses described under rock garden plants grow happily almost anywhere, and are lovely in flower, fruit, and leaf. These are *Rosa foliolosa*, white flowers, and *R. arkansana*, pink. *Conradina canescens*, a

---

* Standard Cyclopedia of Horticulture, L. H. Bailey.

member of the Mint Family, covers sand dunes with feathery glaucous-green foliage. With its tiny leaves, graceful habit, and little lavender or white flowers it is a lovely thing. Small gives it to Florida and Alabama, but it has withstood zero temperatures here at Briarwood.

For large grounds, Fragrant Sumac, *Rhus aromatica*, is attractive, especially in autumn, when it takes on fine shades of red. In the north and northwest, nothing could be finer for covering rocky or sandy slopes than Bearberry—weighed down by the name *Arctostaphylos uva-ursi*. It is a trailing evergreen shrub, bearing small racemes of little red-tinged white flowers, and red berries. It revels in cold, and cannot be grown in the south, except in mountainous regions. Another pretty trailer for northern gardens—or mountains in the south—is Wintergreen, *Gaultheria procumbens*. With small shining leaves, clustered tiny white urns, and bright-red berries, it provides a charming cover for a cool spot. As both these plants belong to the Heath Family they must have acid soil.

Most Oregon plants cannot be grown in other parts of the country, but the *Mahonias* are the exception. They thrive from coast to coast, north and south. *Mahonia repens* is an evergreen creeper, with bronze hues in winter.

There are some attractive species suitable for ground-covers among herbaceous plants. One of the prettiest of these is Creeping Beggartick, *Meibomia michauxii*, with rounded trifoliate leaves, velvety and pink-tinted when young. In fall, dainty sprays of lavender pea-shaped flowers spring from the axils of the leaves. The related Pink Partridge Pea, *Strophostyles umbellatus*, has small trifoliate leaves, and long-stemmed pink flowers, borne in pairs. Butterfly Pea, *Bradburya virginiana*, bears larger flowers of lavender—much prettier than the related *Clitoria mariana*. Both these peas trail over sandy banks, adorned with their charming flowers all late summer and early fall. All three of these species are perennials. Rex Pearce sometimes offers seeds.

One of our showiest perennials is Wild Potato, *Ipomoea pandurata*, which will cover steep banks in poor sandy soil. Of mornings it displays three-inch white flowers with purple throats, and when it is cloudy the "Morning-glories" remain open all day. With its deep, potato-like root, it should be able to withstand considerable cold.

For shady hillsides, Wild Ginger is most attractive, with leathery heart-shaped leaves which are not damaged by cold. *Asarum shuttleworthii* is the finest species, with dark leaves mottled white and lighter green. In early spring, the foliage of *Trilliums* is ornamental, but the leaves die off early.

There is nothing I love more than a carpet of wild Violets beneath trees and shrubs. One that grows well in shade is *Viola papilionaceae*, and colors vary, the type being bright blue. I have a lovely pure white one that comes true from seed. It came, through the Alabama Market Bulletin, from Miss Bonnie Black, Atmore, Alabama. The pretty blue-and-white striped Violet sold as *Viola priceana* is thought to be a form of this species. In her rich red clay at Arcadia, Louisiana, Inez Conger has great mats of dainty *Viola striata*, with cream-colored flowers. It is charming between big flat rocks along a tiny stream.

THE WILD GINGERS. 1. HEXASTYLIS ARI-
FOLIA, SEVERAL TYPES. 2. HEXASTYLIS
SHUTTLEWORTHII, THE MOST ATTRACTIVE
SPECIES. ALL MAKE CHARMING GROUND-
COVERS.

Phlox subulata, so much used in rock gardens, is also
attractive as a ground-cover, and will grow almost anywhere. Creeping Phlox, *P. stolonifera,* with light blue
flowers, succeeds in cool situations, only. Found in the
wild from Georgia to Ohio, it loves mountain slopes,
acid soil, and humus. In the West there are several mat-
forming species, such as white-flowered *P. allysifolia.*

Where it is kept cut back along roadsides, *Verbena tenuisecta* forms lovely carpets. Usually violet, white and pink are seen occasionally. Under the same conditions, *V. venosa* is seen in swathes of brilliant violet. *Verbena canadensis*, lovely lavender, is beautiful in masses. All three of these species will thrive in hot sunny spots, and survive zero temperatures.

A standby for shady locations is *Pachysandra procumbens*, which covers the ground with bright green all winter. It revels in rich soil, either acid or slightly calcareous. It occurs in the wild from Florida to Kentucky, but probably can be grown considerably farther north.

Few plants will grow in deep shade and wet ground, but here a number of native ferns will flourish. The *Osmundas* are big and showy, the Lady Ferns, *Athyriums*, are dainty. These should not be planted in the small garden. On higher ground, exquisite native Maidenhair, *Adiantum pedatum*, thrives. Evergreen Christmas Fern with the terrible botanical name, *Polystichium acrostichoides*, likes a well-drained site, in shade. A larger species, Shield Fern, *Dryopteris marginalis*, grows in similar situations. It is a beautiful species, but is seldom offered in the trade. Both of these prefer heavy rich soil, and are perfectly hardy. In cool spots, one should not overlook the mosses, such lovely fillers tucked in between rocks. Those remarkable Japanese create tiny gardens composed of only mosses and stones.

Gardeners in northern parts of the country can grow the beautiful Ground-pine, which is not a Pine at all, but a *Lycopodium*, related to ferns and mosses. It is a flat, spreading, ferny-looking plant, and is evergreen. It forms a lovely ground-cover on cool shady slopes. It can be grown as far south as North Carolina, in mountainous regions. In approximately the same area is found the Dwarf Cornel, *Cornus canadensis*. It is only a few inches high, with one "dogwood flower," followed by a red berry. When closely planted, it is an attractive ground-cover.

It is not always desirable to grow grasses or other green plants under trees. Beneath pines, the most fitting and beautiful covering is a carpet of soft brown needles, blending with the colors of the tree trunks. And this is a happy choice for it requires no upkeep.

SUMMARY, GROUND-COVERS

Mitchella repens, 4 to 8, and n. parts of 9, east of Neb. Shade, acid.

Dichondra carolinensis, 7 to 9, east of Tex. Sun or shade.

Vinca minor, 3 to 8, shade, dry or damp.

Yellow Jessamine, *Gelsemium sempervirens*, 7 and 8, east of Cen. Tex. Acid soil.

Sand Myrtle, *Leiophyllum buxifolium*, 7 east. Acid sandy soil. Cool sites.

Ceanothus prostratus, 7 and 8, upper Pacific coast regions, only.

Ceanothus fendleri, 4 and 5, west. Dry sandy slopes.

Trailing Arbutus, *Epigaea repens*, 5 to 7, northern parts of 8. Shade, acid.

Rosa foliolosa and *R. arkansana*, 4 to 8, heavy calcareous soils, but will grow in sandy land if lime added.

Bearberry, *Arctostaphylos uva-ursi*, 3 to 7, except in hot or arid regions. Well drained acid soil.

Conradina canescens, 7 to 9, east of Oklahoma. Sandy soil.

Rhus canadensis, (R. aromatica), 4 to 9, east of Nebraska. Well drained site.

Wintergreen, *Gaultheria procumbens*, 3 to 7, east of Illinois. Shade, dry.

Mahonia repens, 5 to 8, sheltered locations.

Meibomia michauxii, 4 to 8, sun or shade, acid sandy soil. Creeping perennial.

Strophostyles umbellata, 5 to 9, east of Kans. Perennial. Sun, sandy soil.

Ipomoea pandurata, 4 to 8, east. Perennial. Sandy soil, sun or shade.

Wild Ginger, *Asarum shuttleworthii*, 7, 8 and n. parts
of 9, east. Shade.

Violets, some species in all zones 4 to 9, except arid
regions.

Phlox subulata, 5 to 8 and n. parts of nine, east. Well
drained sites, sun.

Creeping Phlox, *P. stolonifera*, 5, 6, 7, east. Rich soil.
Cool sites.

Phlox allyssifolia, 4 and 5, west. Well drained sites.

Verbena canadensis, 6 to 9, east. Well drained sites, sun.

Moss Verbena, *V. tenuisecta*, 8 and 9, Fla. to Tex. Sun.
Various soils.

Pachysandra procumbens, 7 and 8, east. Well drained
sites. Shade.

Dwarf Cornel, *Cornus canadensis*, 4 and 5, except arid
regions. Shade.

Ground Pine, *Lycopodium tristachium*, 4 to 7, east of
Neb. Open woods.

Osmundas, large ferns, 4 to 9, east of Cent. Tex. Damp
ground.

Athyriums, some species everywhere, except in arid regions. Wet ground.

Maidenhair Fern, *Adiantum pedatum*, all zones except
in arid regions. Cool sites, rich soil.

Christmas Fern, *Polystichium acrostichoides*, 4 to 9, east
of Nebraska. Rich soil. Shade.

Dryopteris marginalis, 3 to 8, east of Nebraska. Shady
slopes.

Bog Torches; Golden Club; Orontium
aquaticum. (Yellow. Spring).

BY ALL MEANS HAVE POND

Where there is beauty a reflecting pool ·doubles it, so I had to have a pond—not a concrete pool, but a *real* pond, with dirt bottom and sides. I had a tiny spring-fed stream between steep hills, the perfect setting.

First came preparation. A local engineer staked out the boundary, then the tangle of trees, shrubs, and vines was cleared off and stumps dug out. At that time local road work was done with big scoops drawn by mules. I was so fortunate as to catch a road-gang just as they finished a project, and in two days they moved the soil and built the dam. At one end a waste-way was cut to take care of runoff. It took only a few days for the water to come in. I had a pond!

The whole thing had a new raw look, but a year or two would remedy that. On one side was a bank four feet high, and enough brown stones to rock it up and prevent caving. This was slow work, as soil and plants had to be placed between the rocks. Here went native Violets, *Iris cristata, I. verna*, Wild Ginter (*Asarum*, several species) , and small ferns. At the top were planted Mountain Laurels, native Azaleas, and *Pieris nitida*.

On the other side of the pond the ground was flat, with beds of Sphagnum Moss, where bog plants would flourish. The first to go in was lovely Swamp Candles (*Orontium aquaticum*), with big silvery leaves. In very early spring fleshy white stems push up, each topped with a compact spike of brilliant yellow. It is so showy it has been called by various names, one of the nicest of which is Bog Torches. It is related to the Callas; but the spathe is almost invisible.

IRIS TRIPETALA (2 FEET).

Here was the place for the beautiful but exacting Yellow Fringed Orchids. I took them from one of my own bogs, planted them tenderly, and how they did flourish! *Rhexias* loved the spot, and added their dainty pink all summer. Dr. Small sent me a few plants of *Iris tripetala*, from the Atlantic Coast, and they soon formed a sheet of lovely bloom. However, they were not placed near other plants, for they spread rapidly. The flowers are not large but are borne in profusion on two-foot stems. They possess a delicate perfume like that of Grape Hyacinths.

Pickerel Weed (*Pontederia*), Lizard's-tail (*Saururus*), and (*Sagitaria*, several species) are charming reflected in dark water, but these, too, must be kept away from small plants, as they tend to "take over." I did not plant Cattails (*Typha*), for I have seen them completely cover a pond such as mine.

Itea virginica was already there, and in spring this low shrub hangs out its soft white "kitten-tails." By the way, this is a much more appropriate name for it than Virginia Willow, for it is not a Willow, and certainly not restricted to Virginia.

The botanist, W. W. Ashe, saw my sphagnum bogs and said he knew I could grow beautiful *Pinckneya pubens*. He sent me several plants from Florida and they grew like magic—one blooming a little the third year. In five years they were small trees, and in late spring and early summer clothed themselves in velvety pink bracts. This ineffable color reflected in glassy dark water makes an unforgettable picture.

Not quite a bog plant, but liking moisture, Summer-sweet (*Clethra*, two species) was given a place. Fragrant white flowers keep coming all during early summer, and it begins blooming when only two or three feet high. Tingle Nursery offers a pink form which is lovely, and just as sweet as the white. In this same fairly moist location, *Viburnum nudum* was already growing. It is a charming shrub, with broad corymbs of cream-white flowers, followed by berries that are first whitish-green, then pink, and finally blue, with all three colors inter-

PINCKNEYA PUBENS. LOW TREE.

mingled. The leaves are shining green, but are deciduous.

Red Chokeberry, *Aronia arbutifolia*, grew there, too—
a little "leggy" from crowding, but topped back, soon
put out numerous lateral branches. Each of these bears
a tight cluster of flowers like miniature apple blossoms,
followed by brilliant red fruits. Before falling, leaves

are tinted pretty shades of red. Why this attractive shrub is not better known to horticulture is another one of the mysteries, as it will grow in most any location, and begin to bloom and bear when eighteen inches in height. It is offered by a few nurseries.

Plants loved the soft soil of the dam, and soon began springing up here and there. When the pond was being created, many were scooped up and piled on the dam. Closed Gentians had always grown along the little stream, and to my joy they put in their appearance, and a few bloomed the first year. Dainty white violets were there, and soon formed sheets of bloom during early spring. *Rhexias* came in, and small ferns. In two years, *Mitchella repens* carpeted the dam. Nature healed all scars, as she will always do if given half a chance.

As the dam was six feet high, the lower side offered a perfect spot for planting flowering shrubs. There went native azaleas, pink, white, and yellow, and of course, Oakleaf Hydrangea. The lowest level offered an ideal spot for Withe-rod, pretty *Viburnum cassinoides*, with long pointed leaves and panicles of white flowers, followed by fruits showing the same colors as those of *V. nudum*. It grows taller than the latter, so flowers and berries show up prettily above lower shrubs. Here, for winter display, was planted *Ilex longipes*, with long slender branches and small deciduous leaves. Unlike the fruits of other members of the Holly Family, these hang on long stems, are bright red, and form sprays of grace and beauty.

I hated not to put in our beautiful native Waterlilies, the *Nympheaes* and pale-yellow *Nelumbo lutea*, but I knew they would spread rapidly and soon cover the pond in a solid sheet. They are lovely in a concrete pool, where they can be controlled.

Perhaps it is in the fall that the pond attains perfection. The natural bottom is white sand, the clear water has an amber tint, and in deeper parts is black. At the upper end the glassy mirror repeats the glorious color of *Helianthus angustifolia*. It is tall, branches gracefully, and forms masses of bright gold. Above this blaze the Red Maples (*Acer rubrum*), the color contrasting prettily with the white and gray of the slender trunks. There, too, are the Shadblows (*Amalanchiers*), in clear lemon yellow. Higher still, White Hickory and Beech glow golden.

The pond is wide enough that the trees on the hillsides do not shade it too much. In our hot sun most shrubs and herbaceous plants like protection from the blaze of mid-day. Yes, leaves blow into the water at the edges and have to be raked out in late fall. Most of the plants that have been named are hardy much farther north. Twice since the pond was made it was frozen over solidly, for the temperature dropped to zero. Only *Pinckneya pubens* was cut back, and in two years it recovered.

I planned the pond so it would reflect full-length my one huge Longleaf Pine, left over from the primeval forest. There he stands in all his majesty, with his portrait at his feet.

It seemed to me that this little sheet of quiet water would offer a resting place for migrating ducks and geese, so I called it "Wings-rest." Perhaps it is too hidden by the forest on surrounding hills, for not many have paused there. When I pass by in winter, two or three startled ducks fly up, but that is all. In summer, the odd Water-turkey (*Anhinga*) sits on an over-hanging branch and stretches his long black neck down toward the water.

Anyone owning a country place with springs can create a pond at small expense, and nothing will pay richer dividends in true pleasure. If no springs, a well can be put down to supply water. It has now been years since mine was made, and each spring the dainty pink cups of Mountain Laurel look down at themselves in dark water. On the lower side of the dam the Wild Azaleas over-top it with exquisite masses of bloom—pink and white *A. canescens*, and *A. austrina* in every shade of yellow, from the palest to sunset-colored.

Some of the shrubs have grown so much they have crowded out many herbaceous plants, but in November there is still the amazing blue of Closed Gentian. *Mitchella* and various mosses and little white Violets clothe the dam—which no one now recognizes as a dam! At first I had gorgeous Louisiana Irises in sunny spots, but the rabbits loved them as much as I did, so they soon disappeared. The wretches do not care for *Iris tripetala* and *I. virginica*, so I had to be content with these.

SUMMARY, BY ALL MEANS HAVE A POND

Violets, several species, all zones except arid regions.

Iris cristata, 7 and 8 e. Between rocks, shade, rich soil.

Iris verna, 5 to 8 e. Dry soil, between rocks, acid. Sun. Adaptable.

Wild Ginger, *Asarum shuttleworthii*, 6 to 8 e. Shade. Adaptable.

Mountain Laurel, *Kalmia latifolia*, 5 to 8 e. N. part of 9. Acid soil.

Azalea canescens, 7 to 9 e. Well drained acid soil. Humus.

A. austrina, 8 and 9 e. of Tex. Well drained acid soil. Humus.

Pieris lucida (Lyonia nitida), 6 to 9 e. of Okla. Damp acid soil.

Swamp Candles, *Orontium aquaticum*, 5 to 9, acid bogs. East, only.

Yellow Fringed Orchid, *Habenaria ciliaris*, 4 to 9 e. Acid bogs.

Rhexia mariana and *R. virginica*, 4 to 9 e. Low ground, acid.

Iris tripetala, 7 to 9, near coast. Acid bog.

Iris virginica, 3 to 9 e. of Neb. Wet acid soil.

Pickerelweed, *Pontederia cordata*, 3 to 9 e. of Cen. Okla. Acid bogs.

Lizardtail, *Saururus cernuus*, 3 to 9, e. of Neb. Acid bogs.

Arrowhead, *Sagittaria latifolia*. All zones e. of Kans. Acid bogs.

Itea virginica, 7 to 9 e. of Tex. Shrub, damp acid ground.

Pinckneya pubens, 7 to 9 e. of Tex. Small tree, acid bogs.

Summersweet, *Clethra alnifolia*, 5 to 9, e. of Tex. Shrub, acid soil.

SUMMER-SWEET; CLETHRA; WHITE OR PINK.

Viburnum nudum, 6 to 8 e. Damp acid soil. Shrub.
V. cassinoides, 3 to 7 e. Rich acid soil. Small tree.
Red Chokeberry, *Aronia arbutifolia*, 5 to 9 e. Very adapt-
    able. Shrub.
Closed Gentian, *Gentiana saponaria*, 5 to 9 e. of Kans.
    Shade. Damp soil.
Turkeyberry, *Mitchella repens*, 4 to 9 e. of Neb. Dry
    acid soil. Shade.

Helianthus angustifolius, 7 to 9. Acid soil. Very adapt-
    able.

Hydrangea quercifolia, 7 to 9 e. Shrub. Light acid soil.

Ilex longipes, 7 to 9 e. of Tex. Deciduous shrub. Acid
    soil, various sites.

Red Maple, *Acer rubrum*, 3 to 9 e. of Cen. Tex. Well
    drained acid soil. Tree.

Shadblow, *Amalanchier canadensis*, 4 to 9 e. of Neb.
    Small tree.

White Hickory, *Carya alba*, 3 to 9 e. of Colo. Dry sites,
    acid soil. Tree.

Beech, *Fagus grandifolia*, 7, 8, and n. 9 e. of Kans. Big
    tree, acid soil.

THE GLORY OF AUTUMN

Beauty of Foliage and Fruit

Certainly autumn color is the most neglected feature in landscape planting. When looking at glowing trees and shrubs on an October day, I always feel that no flowering tree could be more beautiful. And most of these species will give us of their bounty with almost no care.

Elder, *Sambucus canadensis*, does not wait for fall to take on color, the big panicles of berries turning shining black in August. The showy red fruits of *S. pubens* color in summer, but cling till eaten by birds. Those with sufficient space—especially bird-lovers—should not neglect planting these fine, easily grown shrubs.

The fruits of Beautyberry, *Callicarpa americana*, (often called "French Mulberry") take on their startling magenta-wine in September. As it branches from the ground, there will be many stems strung with berries, very showy. However, care should be taken in placing it, as the odd color clashes with reds. The rough leaves are not attractive and after they fall the plant is much prettier. I cut long stems, clip off every leaf, and arrange in an earthenware pitcher. Sometimes one is so fortunate as to find an albino form in the wild, and the white berries are exquisite. Some of these "come true" from seed in the first generation. This shrub requires no care, and grows in any well drained soil. It occurs from Virginia to Florida and Texas, but probably can be grown farther north, as it can be cut to the ground, and will come up and bear on the current year's wood.

137

The pretty fruits of the wild roses are little known and appreciated. From low shrubs to high-climbing vines, they all bear red berries which turn early. Some are borne in graceful sprays which are attractive when cut and used in arrangements. The large fruits of *Rosa Laevigata* are orange-red, and not shining as those of some species, but are quite ornamental.

I am always shocked when winter visitors to Briarwood ask, "What is that tree with those beautiful red berries?" Dogwood—our common *Cornus florida*, which they have seen all their lives! They know this lovely tree when in bloom, but are not acquainted with its other charms. The shining fruits cling all winter, or until hordes of Yankee Robins swoop down and devour them! Other birds love them too, and I have seen Titmouse holding one down and picking away the bitter meat. As if beautiful blossoms and fruit were not enough, the leaves take on glorious shades of red in autumn.

There are several species of *Cornus* with white fruits and they are quite attractive. *Cornus asperifolia* is found from Canada to Florida to Texas, and is a rather straggling shrub in woodlands, but when planted in the open is much more shapely. On the Natchez Trace Parkway, near Natchez, Mississippi, there are fine specimens, low and twiggy, and bearing masses of white berries with red stems. In some plants the fruits are tinted pink, very lovely. *Cornus stolonifera*, the well-known Red Osier Dogwood, also bears white fruits. This must be hardy all over the north, as it is offered by a number of nurseries. Probably the finest of all is *Cornus racemosa*, sometimes listed as *C. candidissima*, a low dense shrub bearing many heads of white flowers, and in the fall loaded down with white berries. There is a beautiful photograph of it in More Aristocrats of the Garden.* The pedicels are red, which add to the charm of the fruits. The two last are northern species, and probably will not be happy farther south than Appalachian regions.

Most of the *Viburnums* have been described under Flowering Trees and Shrubs, for many of them fill a dual role. The round-topped low tree, *V. rufidulum*, has drooping clusters of berries, rose and blue often mingled. *Viburnum nudum*, to six feet, and *V. cassinoides*, a much taller shrub, both bear broad panicles of fruit, pale green, pink, and blue together. Of the latter, Ernest Wilson said, "It is one of the most lovely of all shrubs."** Happily, it takes well to cultivation. On the other hand, beautiful Hobble-bush, *V. alnifolium*, does not thrive in gardens, but is charming in northern woodlands. I sigh when I look at the drooping panicles of shining red berries of Cranberry-bush, *V. americanum*, for I cannot grow it. It is a northern species, but should thrive in the mountains of the Southeast. As if the lovely fruits are not enough, the prettty lobed leaves turn scarlet and crimson in fall.

In North Louisiana we do have *Viburnum scabrellum*, a big shapely shrub with rounded dentate leaves which take on rich shades of deep red very late in the fall. And pretty little *V. acerifolium* forms a sheet of pink, rose, and lavender when the tall trees overhead are bare. The last two will grow in the poorest sandy soil, but must have good drainage.

A beautiful small tree of northern woodlands is Moun-

* More Aristocrats of the Garden, Ernest Wilson.
** Aristocrats of the Garden, Ernest Wilson.

tain Ash, *Sorbus americana*, with attractive pinnate leaves and big loose panicles of bright red berries. These last color in late summer, but cling for months. We of the Deep South cannot grow this lovely thing, but it is happy as far south as the mountains of North Alabama and Georgia.

There are many attractive Barberries, but one of the showiest and most graceful is *Berberis canadensis*, with racemes of scarlet berries, and bright-red foliage in fall. It is a native of the Alleghenies, but can be grown much farther north.

Plants with white fruits are unusual and always attract attention. One that is well known and often grown in northern gardens is Snowberry, *Symphoricarpos albus* (or *racemosus*). It is a low shrub, bearing masses of snow-white berries in autumn. It is found in the wild all across the north, and to California. It is sold by a good many nurseries. *S. occidentalis* is a similar species, but grows a little taller.

More than thirty years ago Ernest Wilson* wrote, "Among native trees and shrubs undoubtedly the most beautiful are the Hawthorns (*Crataegus*) whose decorative value is not fully realized." Amazingly, this is still true today. Varied in form, flower, and fruit, some species can be found growing in almost every part of the United States. Hardy and adaptable, they will grow in almost any soil, even alkaline, and are especially suited to difficult exposed slopes. The more they have to wrestle with winds, the more interesting the forms, low, gnarled, and twiggy. About the only species that may be had from nurseries, and often planted, is Washington

---

* Aristocrats of the Garden, Ernest Wilson.

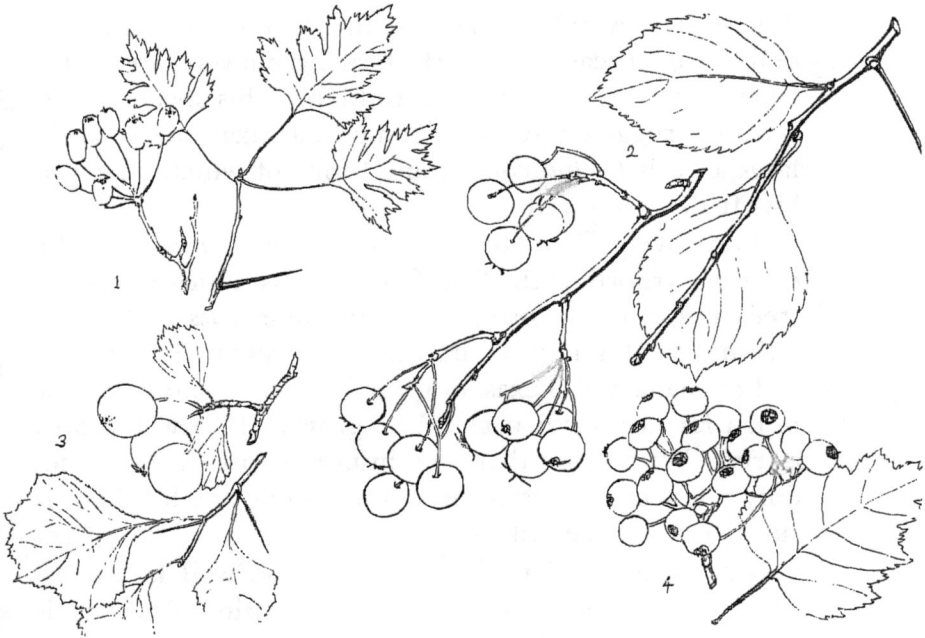

FOUR HAWTHORNS: 1. PARSLEY HAW; CRATAEGUS   MARSHALLII.
    2.   COCKSPUR THORN; C. CRUS-GALLI. 3. BIG HAW; C.
    RAVENELII. 4. WASHINGTON THORN; C. PHAENOPYRUM.

Thorn, *C. cordata*. It is a slender tree, with pretty leaves
and flowers, and masses of small scarlet berries all fall and
winter. Parsley Haw, *C. apiifolia* (or *Marshallii*), is a
big shrub or small tree· with delicately divided leaves,
lovely flowers, and shining red berries. The latter are
ovoid, and edible. A much larger tree, *C. Spathulata*,
also has very small red fruits, but they are round. It loves
the banks of southern bayous, and its masses of brilliant
red against gray Spanish Moss arrest the attention of
observant winter tourists.

Crataegus crus-galli is a rather flat-topped tree, with
shining ovate leaves, and clusters of large red fruits.

There are several varieties in this group, and one is a delightful spreading dwarf, bearing flowers and fruit when not more than three feet high. This species flourishes on rugged claybanks, somewhat alkaline. A fairly large tree is *C. punctata*, some forms of which bear yellow fruits, some red.

The lovely Pomette Blue, *C. brachyacantha*, is the only Hawthorn with blue fruits. It is a medium-sized tree, of spreading form, and when one mass of blue in fall and winter it is an unforgettable sight. It is native to Louisiana and Texas, only, and I wish I could say how much farther north it could be grown. It is well worth a trial. With more than one hundred species described, only a few can be listed here, but among the lot there is surely one just suited to your garden.

Our beautiful American Holly is too well known to need description, and its smaller cousin, Yaupon, is becoming deservedly popular with gardeners. Both these evergreens bear masses of scarlet berries which cling all winter, when not devoured by hungry birds. But the charming deciduous Ilexes are seldom seen in cultivation. Nothing could be more brilliant in the winter landscape than Winterberry, *Ilex decidua*. It begins bearing fruit when only a shrub, but eventually becomes a small tree with many branches. They color in fall, but are more conspicuous after the leaves fall. This is seen in rich alluvial lands, but will grow in almost any soil. A similar species, also known as Winterberry, is *I. verticillata*, a big much-branched shrub. The slender twigs are thickly set with small red berries, quite showy. Its range extends from Canada to Florida to Louisiana, and is the best known of the deciduous species, offered by a number of nurseries.

Little known is the pretty Mountain Winterberry, *Ilex montana*, a shrub with fat scarlet fruits. As the name would indicate, it grows in mountainous regions, from Massachusetts to Georgia, so should be very hardy. A near relative, *Ilex ambigua* (or *caroliniana*), is even lovelier, for the red berries are translucent. The twigs are so slender they droop with the weight of the fruit, exceedingly graceful. Happily for me it is endemic here in the sand hills, for I have never succeeded in moving a plant! Someone should propagate this beautiful shrub by seeds and grafts and make it available to those doing landscaping. Other attractive Ilexes are found in the wild, and deserve a trial in gardens.

A few nurseries offer *Aronia arbutifolia*, but its beauty deserves wider recognition. When not more than a foot high it begins bearing its compact panicles of shining red fruits, which cling all winter. Its natural habitat is an acid bog, but it is most adaptable and will grow in any good garden soil that is not alkaline. Black Choke-berry, *A. melanocarpa*, is attractive, but not nearly so beautiful as its red-berried kin. These shrubs are very hardy and can be grown to Michigan, and even farther north.

A pretty little shrub for planting along streams and at the edges of woodlands is Burning-bush, *Euonymus americana*. The prickly fruits open, disclosing pendant scarlet seeds, and the slender green twigs droop with their weight. It is especially attractive along trails

In the west they have beautiful *Shepherdia*, Buffalo Berry, a shrub bearing panicles of bright red fruits. As it belongs to the Eleagnuses it should be easy to grow, and probably will succeed in mountainous regions in the eastern states where the soil is alkaline. And California has her glorious Toyon, *Photinia arbutifolia*. As the exotic species of Photinia are easy to grow, this subject should not be too difficult.

In September the leaves of the Sumacs turn scarlet, probably the first species to put on bright autumn color. And how vividly they stand out, along roadsides and in open woodlands! The fruits of *Rhus copallinum* become dark brown, but those of *R. glabra* are deep red well into winter. Staghorn Sumac, *R. hirta*, found in the eastern states, is a smaller shrub than the two former, and the dark-red berries are borne in tight upright panicles, hence the "staghorn." It is quite ornamental, and the "horns" are much used in arrangements. All Sumacs spread by stolons, so should be planted only where space is not at a premium.

Poison Sumac is beautiful in autumn, but should be given a wide berth, as it is extremely poisonous, causing a painful rash, and not as well known as Poison Ivy and Poison Oak. The former, *Rhus vernix*, is easily distinguished from other species, for the leaves are like those of Ash, which gives it another common name, Poison Ash. Also, it grows in boggy sites, while the others require well drained soil.

The next tree to show color is Sourwood, *Oxydendron arboreum*, a slender shapely tree. The pointed ovate leaves take on various shades of pink and red, usually coloring evenly over the entire tree. In early fall it sets mountainsides ablaze. It will grow well at the edge of a woodland, but will thrive in full sun if given acid soil with plenty of humus. It occurs in the wild from New Jersey and Pennsylvania south to Florida and Louisiana.

Keeping pace with Sourwood, Blackgum becomes a glowing mass of red in early fall. It is a shapely medium-sized tree, and loves a place on an exposed hillside. There are several species, but the most beautiful is *Nyssa sylvatica*, with shining ovate leaves. It seems to flourish in either sand or clay, but does not like lime. It is difficult to find this desirable tree in a nursery, but if one gets it from the wild, it is wise to select a small specimen, for it has a long taproot that goes straight down.

At the same time that these trees are lighting eastern woods, western mountainsides are glowing with the gold of Aspen, *Populus tremuloides*, which grows in such pure stands that tree lovers travel many miles to view the display. The rounded pointed leaves hang trembling on long stems, giving its botanical name. This lovely tree is found in many parts of the Northern United States, and deserves to be widely planted. Like all Poplars, it is easy of cultivation.

It seems strange that no one plants Hickories for ornament, for there is one species, *Carya alba*, that becomes spectacular when every leaf turns to pure gold. It is easily distinguished from other Hickories, for the leaves are twice as large, and on young trees the bark is very light. It is not for small grounds, for it finally grows to a magnificent size, with graceful drooping branches. It is best grown from the nuts, as the root goes straight down as soon as it sprouts.

Sweetgum. *Liquidambar styraciflua*, is now sold by nurseries, and highly recommended. It is a healthy vigorous tree, eventually growing very large. The star-

shaped leaves begin coloring in mid-fall, becoming more
and more brilliant as the season advances. The range of
tints is amazing, from light yellow to dark purple, with
every shade of red in between. It is easy to please as to
soil, but if one wants the brilliant display, it must be
planted in full sun. It is most striking on a hillside.

For autumn beauty, probably Maples are the most
favored of all trees. Sugar Maple, *Acer saccharum*, is too
well known as the street tree in the north to need description. It becomes a large shapely specimen, and cannot be
placed where space is in demand. It is very hardy and
can be grown almost anywhere in the United States.
Graceful Red Maple, *Acer rubrum*, is better suited to
gardens, as it does not grow so large. Its coloring is
even more beautiful, ranging from light yellow to crimson, varying with different trees. And let no one tell you
otherwise, the color will be the same year after year!
So if taking a small one from the wild, select one with
fine red leaves, and tie a string on it. Few nurseries offer
this lovely tree. As it ages, it assumes the most delightful
"Japanesy" (overworked word!) forms. It is almost in-
dispensable in creating garden pictures, for, with its
light dappled bark and dainty lobed leaves it is charming
all the year. It grows all over the eastern United States,
and some of the Midwest, and is perfectly hardy. *A.
rubrum drummondii* is a larger coast species, known as
Swamp Red Maple. The leaves take on attractive fall
colors, but not as brilliant as the preceding. It is finest
in late winter, when hung with big keys in various shades
of red.

Acer saccharinum differs from the preceding in that
the prettily lobed leaves are silvery-white beneath, par-

ticularly attractive when they turn yellow in fall. It is easy to grow and makes a charming lawn tree. A medium-sized species, *A. pennsylvanicum*, also assumes beautiful clear yellow coloring in autumn. With its dense habit and unusual bark it is a very desirable tree. This bark is smooth dark green, striped white, which gives it the common name, Striped Maple.

Of the species with yellow foliage, *Acer floridanum* (or *barbatum*) is my favorite Maple. The long slightly drooping branches are thickly clothed with prettily cut leaves hanging on long stems. In late autumn the entire tree becomes a clear glowing yellow, which seems to give off light. Here at Briarwood it retains its color till mid-December. If I could possess only one tree, this would be it. A similar, but smaller species is A. *leucoderme*, with fawn-colored bark and dainty leaves. Its autumn coloring is unsurpassed, and when seen against the white sandy banks of a creek is never forgotten. It grows from North Carolina to Florida and Louisiana, but is rare and local in distribution. It takes kindly to gardens, and it is a pity that some nurseryman does not propagate this lovely tree and put it on the market. They nearly all stock the fancy Japanese Maples, but not our beautiful native species!

There are very attractive Maples in the West, usually low growing and especially good for gardens. Mountain Maple, *A. glabrum*, thrives in the Rocky Mountains and the Sierra, and is completely hardy. Vine Maple, *A. circinatum*, is another charming species which is more widely distributed.

Box Elder, *A. negundo*, is so different from other Maples that only by its winged seeds is it recognizable as such. The branches are so brittle they break easily, but it is widely planted because of its ability to withstand drought and cold. The compound leaves do not color as do those of other species, but the immense drooping panicles of straw-colored seeds are oddly attractive.

Few gardeners seem to know that the Shadblows (*Amalanchier*), so exquisite in early spring, are also beautiful in the fall. The prettily veined leaves of *A. canadensis* become clear lemon, while some species mingle red with yellow. Most of the Shadblows are small enough to be grown in the average garden, and no tree lends itself better to the creation of garden pictures.

The stately Beech, *Fagus grandifolia*, assumes clear yellow coloring in autumn, which gradually turns a soft light brown. This is a large tree with drooping graceful branches, and makes a striking specimen on large grounds. It wants acid soil with plenty of humus, but is rather adaptable.

Another species which grows very large, Tulip Tree, *Liriodendron tulipifera*, is attractive in fall, when the odd leaves turn clear yellow.

Two shrubs that glow like sunshine, even when it is raining, are White Buckeye, *Aesculus parviflora*, and Sweet Shrub, *Calacanthus florida*. The five-fingered leaves of White Buckeye are especially beautiful, seeming to radiate light.

NOVEMBER

It is strange that persons call November "dreary," and poets refer to it as "the saddest of the year." The first week or two it is positively flamboyant with blazing

Sweetgums and Maples, and clear gold of Hickory, Shadblow, and Beech. Comes a rain, hard frost, cold wind,
and the air is filled with swirling bright leaves. Then
Witch Hazels are revealed in all their sweetness. As I
write, my woods are misty with the soft-yellow fringy
flowers. The odd little seed vessels clustered along the
stems add interest to cut sprays. It is difficult to understand why horticultural writers (and catalogs) go into
rhapsodies over the Oriental species, not even mention-
ing the native one, when our own is so much more attractive. Emily S. Parcher* is the exception, for she says,
"*Hamamelis virginiana,* beautiful native shrub. Interesting growing habits." Here at Briarwood they range in
color from cream to deep yellow. I cut branches, put
them in a brown pitcher, and the whole room is filled
with the delicate woodsy fragrance.

For some reason the native Witch Hazel is difficult to
transplant, so it is best grown from seed. It must be ad-
mitted that the flowers on some plants are much finer
than others, so a good plan is to tie a string on one with
extra lovely blooms and wait for seeds to mature. It will
be a long wait, for the fruit capsules do not open for a
year! Plant the native Witch Hazel on a hillside, for it
must have perfect drainage. If given lots of humus, it
withstands drought wonderfully. It flowers well under
tall deciduous trees, but has even more blossoms when
it gets more sunlight.

After most trees are bare, Huckleberries display their
charms. *Vaccinium elliottii* is a flat-topped shrub, with
masses of fine green twigs, and tiny leaves that become
shining red in November. If freezes are not too severe

---

* Shady Gardens, by Emily Seaber Parcher.

CLOSED GENTIAN; GENTIANA SAPONARIA.
GENTIANA ANDREWSII VERY SIMILAR.

they cling well into December, and I have cut sprays
for Christmas bouquets. The cultivated Blueberries
originated in the wild and have been bred up to produce
larger fruit, but some nurseries mention the fact that
they are also ornamental shrubs. The largest of the family, Winter Huckleberry (or Sparkleberry), *V. arboreum*, eventually becomes a small tree, but begins bear-

ing when quite small. In the open, it takes on a fine flat-topped form, the gnarled branches very artistic. It is extremely twiggy, and the tiny glistening leaves become rich dark red. The small berries are relished by all birds, and as they cling till eaten, offer a welcome addition to the winter menu. This big one grows on dry hillsides. If taken from the wild a very small one should be selected, as it is rather difficult to transplant. As Huckleberries belong to the Heath Family, of course they must have acid soil.

The most delightful surprise of November is Closed Gentian (both *Gentiana andrewsii* and *G. saponaria*). It is almost a shock to spy a clump of heaven's own blue on the brown bank of a tiny stream. The flowers, in tight terminal clusters, never open, but the color is so beautiful they are forgiven. I have seen it disputed that Gentians bloom so late, but evidently the exquisite Fringed Gentian also comes in November. William Cullen Bryant* wrote:

"Thou waitest late and com'st alone,
When woods are bare and birds are flown,
And frosts and shortening days portend
The aged year is near his end.

Then doth thy sweet and quiet eye
Look through its fringes to the sky,
Blue—blue—as if that sky let fall
A flower from its cerulean wall."

Now Gentians are not garden plants in the strictest sense, but many persons are acquiring country places, with little streams and woodsy areas, where these lovely things

* To a Fringed Gentian, by William Cullen Bryant.

can be grown from seed. These are fine as dust, and should be lightly sifted on a bed of moss. The patient flower lover will have a few blooms in two years, and the clumps increase in size and persist for a long, long time. They thrive in partial shade, but if they have their feet in damp acid soil, they can be grown in full sun.

In planning garden pictures, late fall should not be forgotten. Few things are lovelier than White Buckeye with graceful curving sprays of Wreath Aster beneath— this includes several species of Aster. An *Aronia arbutifolia* is charming with Closed Gentians and ferns at its feet. Both White Birch and Red Maple are exquisite with pale trunks and bright leaves reflected in a pool. The combinations are endless. Little Maple-leaved Viburnum is now a sheet of soft rose beneath leafless deciduous trees. Its unusual color is also lovely with the maroom of White Oak, which holds its leaves very late. Most Oaks are the last trees to color. The finest of these is Scarlet Oak, taking its name from the brilliant red of the prettily cut leaves. One fall, while in North Alabama, I saw it in all its beauty and longed to add it to my woods. I ordered it from a nursery, but it just stands there, longing for its native mineral-rich soil. There are other species that take on attractive colors in autumn. Some days may be dreary, but November can be glorious.

SUMMARY, THE GLORY OF AUTUMN

Elder, *Sambucus canadensis*, 3 to 8, east of Colorado. Big shrub, adaptable.

Red Elder, *S. pubens*, all zones n. of N. Georgia, except arid regions. Shrub.

Blackhaw, *Viburnum rufidulum*, 5 to 8, east of Colo. Low tree. Adaptable.

Viburnum nudum, 6 to 8, east. Shrub. Damp ground, acid.

Viburnum cassinoides, 3 to 7, east. Large shrub. Rich soil.

Viburnum americanum, 4 to 7 east, except arid regions.

Viburnum scabrellum, 6, 8, and N. 9, east. Big shrub. Well drained locations.

Viburnum acerifolium, 4 to 8, except arid regions. Low shrub, dry woods.

Mountain Ash, *Sorbus americana*, 3 to 7, east. Small tree. Well drained soil.

Barberry, *Berberis canadensis*, 5 to 7, east. Low shrub.

Snowberry, *Symphoricarpos albus*, 3, 4, 5, except in arid regions. Low shrub.

Hawthorn, *Crataegus*, many species, some for every zone. Low trees.

Pomette Blue, *Crataegus brachyacanthus*, 8, La. and E. Tex. Low tree.

Winterberry, *Ilex verticillata*, 3 to 8, east. Big shrub, deciduous.

Winterberry, *Ilex decidua*, 6 to 8, big shrub. Likes heavy soil, adaptable.

Ilex montana (*monticola*), 5 to 7, east. Shrub, deciduous.

Red Chokeberry, *Aronia arbutifolia*, 5 to 9, east. Shrub. Adaptable.

Black Chokeberry, *A. melanocarpa*, 5 to 9, east. Shrub.

Euonymus americana, 5 to 9. Slender shrub. Shady woods.

Shepherdia argentia, 4 and 5, west and north. Shrub. Slopes.

Sumac, *Rhus copallina*, 4 to 9, east. Big shrub. Well drained sites.

Smooth Sumac, *R. glabra*, 4 to 9, east. Shrub. Rich dry soil.

Staghorn Sumac, *R. hirta* (*typhina*), 3 to 7, east. Shrub. Dry rich soil.

Sweetgum, *Liquidambar styraciflua*, 6 to 9, adaptable. Large tree.

Sourwood, *Oxydendron arboreum*, 6 to 9, east. Small tree, acid soil.

Blackgum, *Nyssa sylvatica*, 4 to 9, east. Large tree. Hillsides.

Aspen, *Populus tremuloides*, 4 to 6, except arid regions. Medium tree.

White Hickory, *Carya alba*, 3 to 9, east of Colo. Large tree. Hills.

Sugar Maple, *Acer saccharum*, 3 to 8, east. Large tree. Very adaptable.

Red Maple, *Acer rubrum*, 3 to 9, east of Cen. Tex. and Nebraska. Dry woods.

Swamp Red Maple, *A. rubrum drummondii*, 6 to 9, east of Okla. Low ground.

Silver Maple, *A. saccharinum*, 3 to 8, east of Colo. Medium tree. Adaptable.

Striped Maple, *A. pennsylvanicum*, 5 to 7, east. Small
   tree.

Sou. Sugar Maple, *A. floridanum*, 4 to 9, east. Medium
   tree, adaptable.

Acer leucoderme, 7 to 9, east. Small tree. Sandy soil.

Boxelder, *Acer negundo*, all zones. Medium tree. Adaptable.

Mountain Maple, *A. circinatum*, 3 to 7, west. Beautiful
   small tree.

Mountain Maple, *A. glabrum*, 3 to 7, west. Shrubby tree.

Shadblows, *Amalanchier*, some species in every zone.
   Shrubs to small trees.

Beech, *Fagus grandifolia*, 4 to 9, east of Kansas. Big tree.
   Acid soil.

Tuliptree, *Liriodendron tulipifera*, 3 to 8, east. Large
   tree. Adaptable.

White Buckeye, *Aesculus parviflora*, 7, 8, east. Shrub.
   Very adaptable.

Sweetshrub, *Calacanthus floridus*, 7 to 9, east. Shrub.
   Adaptable. Dry soil.

Witch-hazel, *Hamamelis virginiana*, 4 to 9, east of Cent.
   Okla. Big shrub.

Huckleberry, *Vaccinium elliotii*, 7, 8, east of Cent. Tex.
   Shrub.

Winter Huckleberry, *V. arboreum*, 6 to 9, east of Cent.
   Kans. Small tree.

White Oak, *Quercus alba*, 4 to 9, E. of Cen. Kans. Big
   tree.

Scarlet Oak, *Q. coccinea*, 5 to 7, east of Cen. Mo. Large
   tree. Rich soil.

Closed Gentian, *Gentiana andrewsii*, 4 to 7, E. of Kans.
   Perennial.

Sou. Closed Gentian, *G. saponaria*, 5 to 9, east of Kans.
    Damp ground.
Fringed Gentian, *G. crinita*, 4 to 7, east. Damp ground.
Fall Asters, some species in every zone, various soils.

WINTER

When someone remarks, "Winter looks so dead," I am always shocked. The trees are by no means dead, merely sleeping, and only after the falling of the leaves is their beautiful architecture revealed. Then even Sycamores are endurable. I hate them in summer, but when I see their snow-white branches against a blue sky, I relent.

A flowering tree could not be more beautiful than a Beech in winter, especially on a damp misty day. The smooth bark is dappled white and soft gray, and on the north side there are always lichens. Lichens are lovely at all times, but when wet they take on delicate shades of pale green. The long slender branches are very graceful, and twigs are tipped with brown satin buds.

The massive branching of oaks is fascinating, especially White Oak, *Quercus alba*, with its pale bark. In age, White Hickory, *Carya alba*, also presents interesting architectural designs. The slender silver-dappled trunks and branches of Red Maple are lovely in winter. Famous *Betula papyrifera* is so white it is almost startling, but exquisite in the landscape. The last is for northern states, only.

The massing of bare twigs in various patterns is a characteristic feature of some species. The limbs of Water Oak, *Quercus nigra*, form twiggy masses which are attractive against an evening sky. The majestic White Elm, *Ulmus americana*, becomes a giant fan of graceful branches. As a winter tree, Winged or Cork Elm, *Ulmus alata*, is even more beautiful. It seems to

157

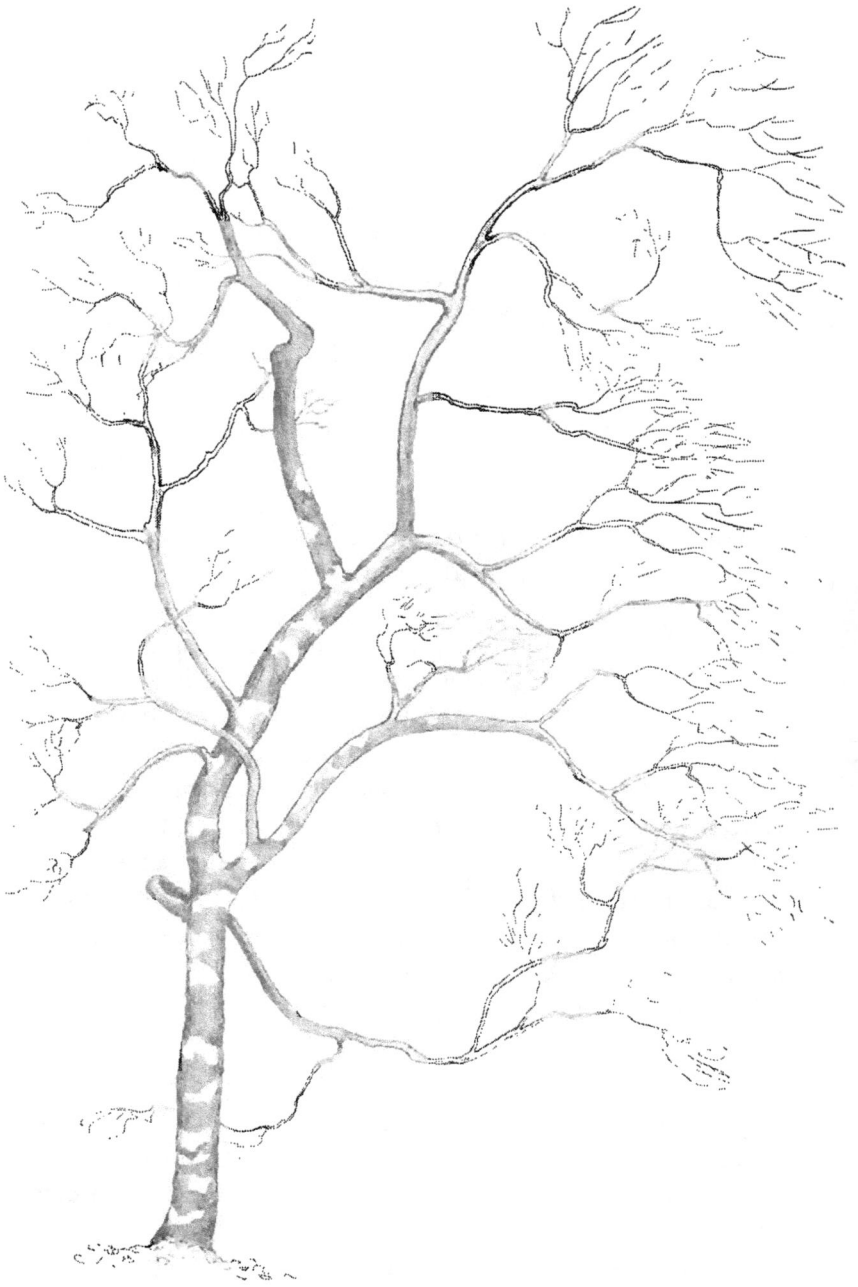

SHADBLOW IN WINTER.

be little known, but when seen is much admired. In January, the stems are clothed in tiny seeds, like clouds of lavender smoke. The slender branches are "weeping," and a large specimen is impressive. One thing that should be kept in mind regarding Elms, they are all very intolerant, devour the soil, so shrubs and herbaceous plants will not flower when planted beneath them.

The corky "wings" on twigs of Sweetgum (*Liquidambar*) and Winged Elm make interesting winter studies, and are often used in flower arrangements. Many trees and shrubs put on their buds in late summer and early fall, and this adds charm to Dogwood, Wild Azalea, and other species.

On a sparkling cold day I am always entranced by the glistening twigs of the little-known Sloe (*Prunus umbellata*). They are deep purple, and shine in the sun as if coated in ice. And when it snows they become airy clouds of white. This is true, also, of Winter Huckleberry, with its masses of fine twigs. When covered with snow, the conifers are supreme in their beauty, but many deciduous trees are attractive, too. Then the pretty seed-cups of Tulip Tree (*Liridendron*) are like white flowers. Linden is a graceful tree in the winter landscape.

The colored branches of some shrubs add beauty to the winter scene. Clumps of Osier Dogwood, *Cornus stolonifera*, with slender red twigs, are most attractive. It is found all across the northern states, and is sold by nurseries. Alas, however, it refuses to take on its pretty color where winters are mild.

COMMON WITCH HAZEL; HAMAMELIS VIRGINIANA,
SWEETENS THE WOODS IN DECEMBER.

ILEX CASSINE ANGUSTIFOLIA.

A number of trees and shrubs hold their fruits into winter. All of the *Ilexes* retain their bright berries till spring, those that lose their leaves being most conspicuous. *Ilex decidua* is like a flame against bare branches of others trees, and can be made a focal point in a landscape. Dogwoods and some of the *Viburnums* are also attractive.

SUMMARY, WINTER

Beech, *Fagus grandifolia*, 4 to 9, east of Kans. Large tree, Acid soil.

White Oak, *Quercus alba*, 4 to 9, east of Cen. Kans. Large tree, hills.

Scarlet Oak, *Q. coccinea*, 5 to 7, east of Mo. Large tree, rich soil.

White Hickory, *Carya alba*, 3 to 9, east of Colo. Large tree, hills.

Red Maple, *Acer rubrum*, 3 to 9, east of Nebraska. Medium tree, hills.

White Birch, *Betula papyrifera*, 3 to 7, from Atlantic to Pacific.

Water Oak, *Quercus nigra*, 6 to 9, east of Cen. Oklahoma. Adaptable.

White Elm, *Ulmus americana*, 3 to 9, east of Colo. Fine tree, adaptable.

Winged Elm, *Ulmus alata*, 6 to 9, east of Cen. Okla. Beautiful tree.

Sweetgum, *Liquidamber*, 5 to 9, except in arid regions. Large tree.

Sloe, *Prunus umbellata*, 7 to 9, east of Cen. Tex. Low tree. Hills.

Tuliptree, *Liriodendron tulipifera*, 5 to 8, east. Large tree. Rich soil.

Osier Dogwood, *Cornus stolonifera*, 3 to 6, east to west. Shrub, red twigs.

Flowering Dogwood, *Cornus florida*, 5 to 9, east of Cen. Tex. Small tree.

Winterberry, *Ilex verticillata*, 3 to 9, east of Nebraska. Big shrub.

Southern Winterberry, *I. decidua*, 7 to 9, east of Cen. Okla. Large shrub.

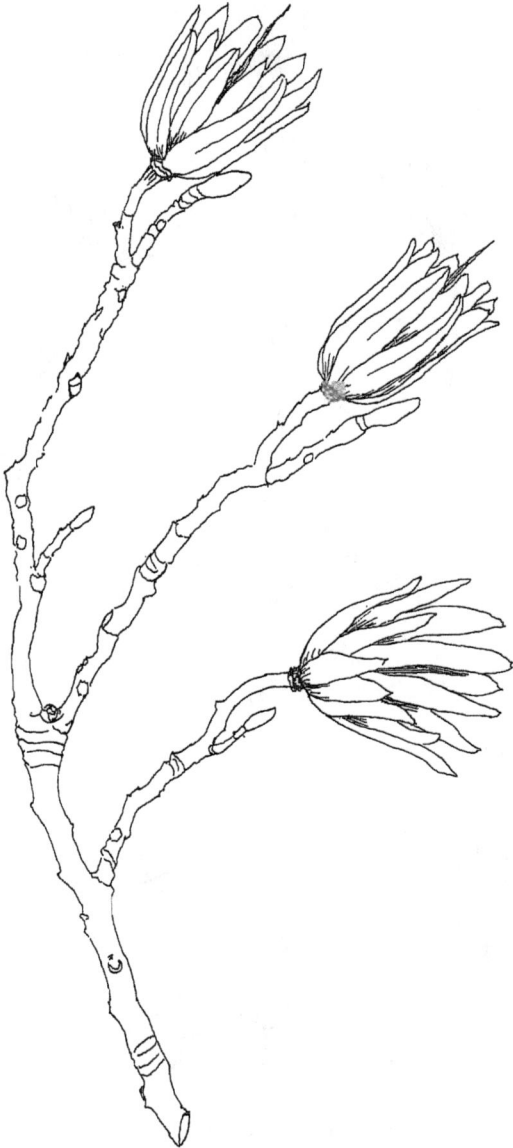

SEED-CUPS OF TULIP TREE.

CENTAURIA AMERICANA.

GROW WILD FLOWERS FROM SEED

If there is one thing with which I have no patience it is an *im*patient gardener. Often I am told, "I can't wait to grow things from seed!" Well, *I* am still planting seed, and waiting happily to see them produce flowering plants. This is by far the best way to grow the spectacular *Magnolia macrophylla*, for it is difficult to transplant. Like seeds of all Magnolias, the oily covering must be thoroughly washed off. These should be gathered as soon as the fruits open, and planted at once. Those who do not grow plants from seed are missing a thrilling experience. And growing them thus leaves one conscience-free, for then there is no need to tear them from their chosen haunts.

All who see my blaze of Scarlet Gilia in June want it, and if they own a sandy, sunny spot, I gladly give them seed. The first time I saw it in the scrub-oak country of East Texas I thought the woods were on fire! The stems rise two to six feet, with a plume of scarlet flowers topping each. Locally, it is called "Texas Plume," a rather nice common name. The seeds should be broadcast as soon as they mature in early fall, but the first year they make only feathery green tuffets, so no mowing. Biennials, they bloom the second year, then die, so I sow a fresh crop every year.

While on the subject of Texas wild flowers, we may as well discuss the lovely Texas Bluebell, *Eustoma russellianum*, certainly one of the most beautiful flowers on earth. It belongs to the Gentians, but is quite different from other members of the family. The stiff stem usually has a number of branches, each tipped with a three-inch

saucer-shaped flower in shades of lavender-blue. Some
are violet, with a white zone around a black center,
and yellow anthers. The fact that the flowers keep well
when cut has doomed this wonderful plant—unless
flower lovers act. Although Texas has a law against
cutting or digging native plants, florists cut the Bluebells
by the truck-load, and ship them all over the country.
There used to be acres of them, presenting an unforgettable picture, but these are fast vanishing. If florists
want them, let them grow them from seed! Mrs. Oscar
Shanks (Pineville, La.) has flowered them thus, and
there are probably others. The seeds are fine as dust,
and are rather difficult—but surely worth any amount of
trouble. These are habitants of the Black Lands, so
demand heavy alkaline soil.

Another spectacular Texas flower (Texas has many)
is *Eryngium leavenworthii*, and it, too, is disappearing.
The branching plant, 2 to 4 feet high, has pretty glaucous
leaves, but beware, for each lobe is tipped with a sharp
spine. I know this can be grown from seed, for I did it,
and painted it. Someone wheedled me out of the painting, so when I needed it for my Flowers Native To The
Deep South, I had to collect a specimen. I rode a thousand miles with those prickles sticking my legs, for the
car was full of people, with little room for plants. I
bought a bucket, put a little water in the bottom, and
wrapped the flowers in newspaper—but the spines went
right through. I painted it again—but please don't
ask me to do it over! It defies description, but in late
summer, the entire plant begins turning purple, and by
fall, is brilliant violet. How the flower arrangers should
love it, for it retains this startling color for months. It,

too, grows in the alkaline Black Lands, but is more adaptable than *Eustoma*. Alas, I cannot find anyone who collects seed of these beautiful Texas flowers! Sometimes Rex Pearce offers them for sale.

For some reason, Texas Bluebonnet (*Lupinus texanum*) has caught the popular fancy, and is better known than the more showy Bluebell. It is lovely when blue acres—no, miles—of it roll away in the distance. But this is the way it is effective, in masses. The seed should be broadcast as soon as they mature, and will form nice little tuffets before winter. (This is true of most wild flower seed.) Bluebonnets like a sandy soil, on the alkaline side. All the Lupines should be grown from seed, as most are either annuals or biennials. Two exceptions are the coastal species, *L. perennis* and *L. diffusus*, which form sheets of lovely blue on sunny sandy beaches. I wish I knew a source of seeds of these two beauties.

Instead of digging up a few specimens, it is so much more fun to gather seeds, and have masses of a desired plant. It is difficult to find them when not in flower, so it is safer to tie strings, or mark them in some other way. Then one must visit them often, for some species dehisce and scatter their seed far and wide. In a sunny cutover area, I found a garden of the delightful *Echinaceae pallida*—the flowers so much more graceful than the rather heavy *E. purpurea* (sold as *Rudbeckia purpurea*). I carefully marked the spot, gathered seed at the proper time, and now *I* have them in sunny spots here at Briarwood. Their native site is in heavy clay, but they are most adaptable, and grow and bloom in my acid sandy soil.

The related *Rudbeckia hirta* (annual) is a little coarse, but makes a gay showing on large grounds, providing sheets of bright gold on hot June days. The seeds mature in late summer, and may be scattered in sunny spots. *Rudbeckia triloba* is a more showy species, with branching stems up to six feet, each tipped with a bright yellow flower. Only the lower leaves are tri-lobed, making it a bit difficult to identify when in bloom. It is a perennial, and the clumps become handsomer each year. The drying leaves are delightfully aromatic. *Rudbeckia maxima* has big beautiful glaucous leaves, mostly basal, but the plant lacks the grace of *R. triloba*. The stems are quite tall, sometimes eight feet, topped with large flowers, with drooping yellow ligules.

A related species, *Helianthus angustifolius*, is a showy perennial, and why it is not in the trade is difficult to understand. It branches from the ground up, each slender stem tipped with a bright yellow flower, and is grace itself. It grows in masses in sunny spots along roadsides, and nothing makes a braver showing in fall. It is easy to transplant, still easier from seed, and will grow almost anywhere.

It is much more satisfactory to raise the various *Liatris* species—some called Gayfeather—from seed than to snatch up the corms. They will live if given any care at all. But they grow readily from seed, and then one can have sheets of them, and that is the way they are effective. They will thrive in any well drained soil, but require sun.

When seen in masses, *Centauria americana* is very showy. On prairies of Oklahoma, it grows along roadsides for miles, and is beautiful. From three to five feet tall, it bears large fluffy flowers of lavender and violet. Full sun. Adaptable as to soils.

Penstemons are fascinating. Here in the South our loveliest is white *P. digitalis,* easily distinguished by the swelling throats. It can be transplanted, but—once again —why not gather seed, scatter in a favorable spot, and have masses of them? The stems are only two or three feet tall, and the racemes of white flowers quite showy. Anyone who has seen a sheet of them in blow (as the late Alice Lounsbury would say) will long to have the same picture. They seem to grow in any soil, but their chosen site is in low heavy ground.

Now there is one red Penstemon, *P. Murrayanus,* found in Texas, and (rarely) in Louisiana. The perfoliate leaves alone, are ornamental, for they are light glaucous-green, the perfect foil for the red of the blossoms. As a last touch, the stems are soft violet. Now this is one of the demanding species, and positively refuses to grow in my acid sandy soil. One day I was at May Nichol's, pouring her brownish sand through my fingers —it fascinates me, for it never packs. Suddenly I exclaimed, "May, I know you can grow Red Penstemon, for it grows in soil exactly like yours!" So we climbed in the car, drove to the "Penstemon Place," and found the seeds exactly right. We gathered some and she sowed them in a sunny spot. They were soon up, and formed pretty green rosettes the first year. The next, she had a real display—branching stems up to four feet, topped with spikes of red flowers. Her sand is deep, slightly on the alkaline side. I have learned the hard way it will grow in no other, but those who possess similar sites can have this showy plant.

There are the western species of *Penstemon,* in every color but yellow, many of them very beautiful. I have grown several, but alas, they do not persist. Claude Barr and others offer a number of species which are well worth trying. Grow them from seed, and if they bloom just one year you will feel well rewarded. Gardeners who live in areas where they are endemic grow them in gardens.

Three little "Iris cousins" (bulbous) come readily from seed, and bloom the second year. They are becoming rare in the wild state, and flower lovers can thus preserve them from extinction. *Nemastylis* wants heavy soil, but is adaptable. *Eustylis* grows in sand with plenty of humus. The third, *Herbertia*, likes fairly low ground, heavy soil. All three are exquisite in the rock garden— or anywhere else.

Don't be prejudiced against Evening Primroses because you do not care for the tall, rather coarse *Oenothera biennis,* for there are many species. One which has eased in from Texas is *O. rhombipetala,* which gladdens my heart on summer mornings with its sheet of sulphur-yellow flowers. The plants are very branching, only about two feet tall. It prefers sandy soil, but is adaptable, and grows readily from seed. A biennial, it blooms the second year.

Our roadsides are becoming beautiful with masses of white and pink *Oenothera speciosa (Hartmannia)*, a perennial. It is easy to grow and a little invasive, so should not be planted where it might crowd out less hardy species. It blooms most of the summer, and the three-inch flowers remain open all day.

The many lovely *Silenes* are better grown from seed as they dislike being moved. I was so fortunate as to find the rare *S. subciliata,* with big flowers of spectrum red. I took one plant, and from that have grown many from seed, as they germinate readily in the open. It is very adaptable as to soil, and will endure cold down to zero. This one is fairly tall but most species are low-growing, therefore perfect rock garden plants. These may be had from nurseries dealing in native plants.

While she was living, my sister-in-law, Ruth Dormon, grew acres of wild flowers from seed—not just ordinary wayside species, but rare and hard-to-get beauties. Beneath her tall trees were drifts of delicate Shooting-stars, big clumps of Celestials (*Nemastylis*), *Silenes*, and sheets of the lovely Ozark Phlox. Gardeners who do this are helping to preserve our fast-vanishing native flora.

Lovely flowers that can be grown from seed, *only*, are the Figworts, for they are parasitic on roots of other plants. The various species of Purple Gerardia—misnamed, for they are pink and rose—bear bignonia-shaped small blossoms on hair-like stems, and are exquisite. I scattered seeds in a favorable spot, and enjoyed them for years. The well known Indian Paintbrush (*Castilleja*) of western prairies, belongs to the same family, and has similar habits. There are a number of Yellow Gerardias, with much larger flowers than the pink species. Some are tall and erect, others low and rather spreading in growth habit. They are very showy in late summer and fall.

One of our showiest wild flowers is also very accommodating, and can be grown in gardens. The late Mrs. Cammie Henry, of Melrose Plantation (Louisiana), had placed faucets so her Louisiana iris could be flooded when needed. I took her several plants of Cardinal Flower, telling her to take special care of them, as they were disappearing from the wild. A few years later, she laughingly said, "Come here, I want you to see your rare flowers!" The *Lobelias* had reseeded themselves, and glowed in masses all through the iris garden. All they ask is some moisture in the growing season.

Nothing could be more fascinating than growing the beautiful Louisiana irises from seed, for often the hybrids are lovelier than their parents. As soon as fruits turn yellow, they should be gathered and seed planted. They bloom the second year. They ask for rich soil, and a fair amount of moisture.

Plant seeds, and know the joy of anticipation.

SUMMARY,
GROW WILD FLOWERS FROM SEED

Magnolia macrophylla, 4 to 9 east. Sheltered sites. Shade while young.

Scarlet Gilia, *Gilia rubra,* 7 to 9 east of Cen. Tex. Sandy land. Sun.

Texas Bluebell, *Eustoma russellianum,* 7 to 9. Heavy alkaline soil. Sun.

Eryngium leavenworthii, 7 to 9. Heavy alkaline soil. Sun.

Bluebonnet, *Lupinus texensis,* 5 to 9. Deep sand, slightly alkaline. Sun.

Lupinus perennis, 5 to 9 east. Deep sand. Sun.

Lupinus diffusus, 7 to 9 east. Deep sand. Sun.

Echinaceae pallida, 4 to 9, east and west. Heavy dry soil. Sun. Adaptable.

Rudbeckia hirta, probably in every zone from 4 south. Dry soil.

R. triloba, 5 to 8 east of Colo. Very adaptable as to soils. Sun.

Helianthus angustifolius, 5 to 9, east and west. Adaptable as to soil. Sun.

Liatris, some species in all zones. Very adaptable.

Penstemon digitalis, 4 to 9, probably e. and w. Adaptable. Sun or shade.

P. murrayanus, Texas and La. Deep alkaline sand. Sun. Probably in other states.

Penstemon species, western. Some in every zone, lovely and varied.

Celestials, *Nemastylis geminiflora,* 4 to 7. Heavy soil, but adaptable.

Eustylis purpurea, 7 to 9, east. Sandy acid soil. Sun or shade.

Herbertia caerulea, 8 to 9 east. Low ground. Sun.

Oenothera speciosa, 5 to 9, from Ari. to N. C. Adaptable. Sun.

O. rhombipetala, Tex. and La. probably other sts. Deep sand. Sun.

Silene subciliata, La. and Tex., probably other sts. Rich soil. Semi-shade.

Shootingstars, *Dodecatheon,* some species in zones from 4 s. Semi-shade.

Phlox, some species in every zone from 4 s. Sun or shade.

Cardinal Flower, *Lobelia cardinalis,* 3 to 9, e. of cen. Tex. Moist ground.

Verbena, some species in every zone from 4 s. Adaptable. Sun.

Purple Gerardia, 5 to 9, east of Tex. Dry sunny sites.

Indian Paintbrush, *Castilleja coccinea.* 5 to 8, e. of Colo. Heavy soil. Sun.

Centauria americana. In all zones from 5 Sou. Annual, 3 to 5 ft. Full sun. Almost any soil.

THE WILD IRIS

Irises are so different from other plants they require a chapter of their own. They have rootstocks, some quite fleshy, so should not be classed with true bulbous plants. They are so lovely they merit a place in all gardens. It is a confused genus, and species have been shuffled about and given one name after another, so if looking for them in catalogs, one should watch for these changes.

The smallest of the family, *Iris verna* and *I. cristata*, have been described under rock garden plants. They differ from all other eastern species, as they will grow in dry situations. The next in size among eastern Irises is a little known gem, *I. brevicaulis*. The flat five-inch flowers are found in lovely shades of bright blue, rarely pure white. When in bloom, the leaves are only a few inches tall and do not hide the flowers, but later become six to ten inches in height. It is a charming plant for a low border. It wants acid soil full of humus, and likes moisture during the growing season. It is found in marshy places in Louisiana, so is grouped with the Irises of that name.

A pretty thing for the edge of a pool is *Iris tripetala*— a misleading name, for it is the sepals that are showy, the petals tiny. The crisp flowers are only three inches across, but borne in such profusion they make a pretty picture reflected in water. The bright lavender flowers are daintily marked in the center, and have the perfume of Grape Hyacinths. I know of no catalog that offers it, but it can be looked for in sandy bogs in pinelands from North Carolina to Florida.

THREE TYPES OF LOUISIANA IRIS.

In similar situations farther north, *I. prismatica* is found. It grows taller than *I. tripetala*, and the delicate flowers are more the familiar Iris form. As the name suggests, they are exquisitely marked with several shades of lavender-blue, white, and yellow. This is another plant lovely for edging pools, and may be had from several nurseries. It grows in wet lands from Canada to North Georgia. Another species found in similar sites is *I. versicolor*, with four-inch violet flowers borne on two-foot stems. It is widely distributed, from Canada to Georgia to Mississippi. *Iris virginica* is a very varied species, some bearing quite small flowers, others are often five inches across. They are extremely graceful in form, with very long claws. In color they range from pure white, through several shades of lavender and pink, to rich violet. With its branching stems, it is floriferous and showy, and so graceful that no other Iris is so lovely as a cut flower. It thrives in wet acid soil, but should never be planted near more delicate species as it is a rampant grower and spreader.

In the West, *Iris missouriensis* is widely distributed, from the Dakotas southward. It bears bright lavender flowers on two-foot stems, and is found in low wet ground. But the most beautiful of western Irises are the dwarf species of Oregon and California, such as *I. tenax, I. purdyi, I. bracteata*, and others. *Iris douglasiana* is a little taller, to two feet. These species display lovely colors, including yellow, various shades of lavender and violet, and many are beautifully veined. They hybridize freely, and growers have produced some outstanding named varieties. Like their dwarf cousins of the East, *I. verna* and *I. cristata*, they like dry situations. They

ask for loose soil with plenty of humus. Oddly enough,
they do not like to be moved while dormant, but should
be taken up in very early spring, just when new growth
is beginning. Best of all is to grow them from seed, and
they begin to flower the second year, and thereafter form
attractive clumps. Alas, like most western plants, they
are difficult in the East, and here at Briarwood, they never
bloom after the first year.

The queen of all native species, the Louisiana Iris, is
unbelievable in its range of color, from pure white,
yellow, pink, clear reds, through every shade of lavender,
to black-violet. In point of size, they are just as amazing,
ranging from the little *I. brevicaulis* to *I. giganticaerulia*,
with five-foot stems. I think I may safely state that never
before was so gorgeous a flower brought straight from
the wilds to gardens.

When Dr. J. K. Small discovered these fields of wonderful Irises in 1935, he made arrangements to come back
year after year to collect and study them. There was
nothing like them in all the world, and in his enthusiasm
he named and described about one hundred as new
species. Since that time, most botanists have disagreed
with him on this, but there are two which stand unchal-
lenged, *I. brevicaulis* (*Hexicaulis*, Small) and *I. giganti-
caerulea*. The seven-inch flowers of the last are usually
some shade of lavender or violet, but occasionally pure
white forms occur, and rarely a rose one is found. The
flowers are delicately fragrant, and shaped more or less
like those of bearded Iris. The other undisputed species,
I. fulva, was discovered many years ago, and when described and painted, created quite a sensation, for it was
an entirely new color in Irises. It is usually brick-red,

but varies to true red and orange-pink. However, the petals and sepals droop and flowers are small, so it has little garden value.

A few flower-lovers in New Orleans ventured into the swamps and brought some fine varieties into cultivation. The late Mary Swords Debaillon of Lafayette explored widely and introduced many lovely ones, most of which were of a surprising flat form. A few florists in New Orleans cut these, calling them Japanese Iris! At Houma, almost to the Gulf, Randolph Bazet found new varieties. Audubon* was the first to call them Louisiana Iris, featuring a pink one in his painting of Parula Warbler.

Hybridizing did not begin in earnest until W. B. McMillan, of Abbeville, discovered great bogs filled with Iris bearing huge flowers of soft yellow and every shade of red. This was an entirely new area, and they were different. Sepals and petals were very broad, with no claws, so the rich colors were displayed in a striking manner.

Some varieties right from the wild were so beautiful they were given horticultural names and put on the market. There were two outstanding whites: Jeune Fille, with recurved segments, exquisitely frilled; and Wild Swan, with wide-winged eight-inch flowers. Kraemer Yellow was pure aureolin. From the Abbeville area came Bayou Vermilion, with big carmine blooms, and Haile Selassie of deep velvety red-violet. Soon collectors with a horticultural bent had crossed the many fine varieties and produced flowers of amazing size, color, and form.

Because these Irises came from swamps, the idea has prevailed that they are bog plants, only. Nothing could

* Birds of America, John James Audubon.

be more erroneous. It is true they are lovely planted by water, as Jo Evans has hers, bordering a small crescent-shaped lake in Northeast Louisiana. But they are also proven garden plants. Inez Conger grows them beautifully right along with Phlox, Delphinium, Hemerocallis, and other perennials. They demand acid soil and abundant humus, but also revel in manure and cottonseed meal. They even tolerate commercial fertilizers. If it becomes dry they ask for water, but here in the South, winter is their growing season, when rainfall is sufficient. They should be transplanted in September. Their cold-resistance is amazing, and they have been grown successfully to New England. They thrive in almost every state, from North Carolina to California— most especially California. They flourish in New Zealand and Australia. They are easily grown from seed, flowering the second year.

A word of warning: the Old World *Iris pseudacoris* is sometimes advertised as "yellow Louisiana Iris." It has escaped and is found in ditches along roadsides. The erect leaves are rather attractive, but it is a sparse bloomer. It is a rampant grower, so should never be planted near less vigorous species. The rather small yellow flowers have black markings, and so easily distinguished from the Louisiana species. With its branching habit and long very slender seed vessels, it more nearliy resembles *I. virginica*.

SUMMARY, THE WILD IRIS

Iris verna, 7 to 8 E. Dry slopes. Sun.

I. cristata, 5 to 8. Rich soil. Shade. Slopes.

I. tripetala, 7 to 9 E. Acid bog. Lovely near water.

I. prismatica, 4 to 7 E. Wet ground.

I. versicolor. All across North. Damp ground.

I. virginica, 5 to 9 E. Damp acid soil.

I. missouriensis, Montana, S. Dakota, SW to Arizona. Damp ground.

I. tenax, Northwest Coast states. Dry soil.

I. purdyi, Northwest Coast States, Dry soil.

I. bracteata, Northwestern Sts. Dry soil.

I. douglasiana, Cal. Adaptable in western states. Dry soil.

Louisiana Irises can be grown in every state, if given acid soil, humus. Light protection in winter, north. Like manure.

I. pseudacoris. NOT native, but often sold as such because it has escaped along ditch banks. Damp ground. Very invasive.

SET THE TABLE FOR THE BIRDS

The simplest way to feed birds is to *plant* their food. There are various shrubs and trees that supply berries almost around the year, and many of these add beauty to the home grounds. Of course in very cold weather, when insects are gone, some protein food will have to be provided. Most bird lovers keep a supply of nut meats, suet, cornbread, etc., available during winter.

Those with sufficient space can grow Wild Cherry, Mulberry, and Elder, which will be alive with songbirds all summer. Huckleberries are pretty shrubs, and some species ripen their fruits quite early. The brambles— blackberry, raspberry, dewberry, etc.—supply welcome food, but these have to be watched lest they "take over." Where space is limited, anyone can grow Pokeberry, and make Mockingbirds, Thrushes, and most all the feathered neighbors happy. The wine-red stems and racemes of shining berries are attractive, and the fruit holds well into autumn.

Elder, *Sambucus* (several species), carries over into early fall, and birds continue to feast on the panicles of pretty berries. *Sassafras* is a tree that is easy to grow, but seems to be little known. It is one of the three trees that carry entire, mitten-shaped, and three-lobed leaves on the same individual. The pretty berries, borne in graceful sprays, ripen early, and are snapped up so fast by the birds one scarcely gets to see them. Happily, they eat only the blue berry, leaving the bright red calyx. The whorls of magenta-wine fruits of Beautyberry, *Callicarpa*, attract some birds, but they seem to prefer the form with white berries.

SASSAFRAS.

After leaves fall, displaying the beautiful red berries, Dogwood, *Cornus florida*, attracts many birds. Although very bitter, these fruits are greatly relished. In the South, Robins come in by the hundreds, and soon strip the trees. The white-fruited Dogwoods also offer welcome food. The Blackgums supply feasts for winter. If given acid soil, two species, *Nyssa sylvatica* and *N. biflora*, are easily

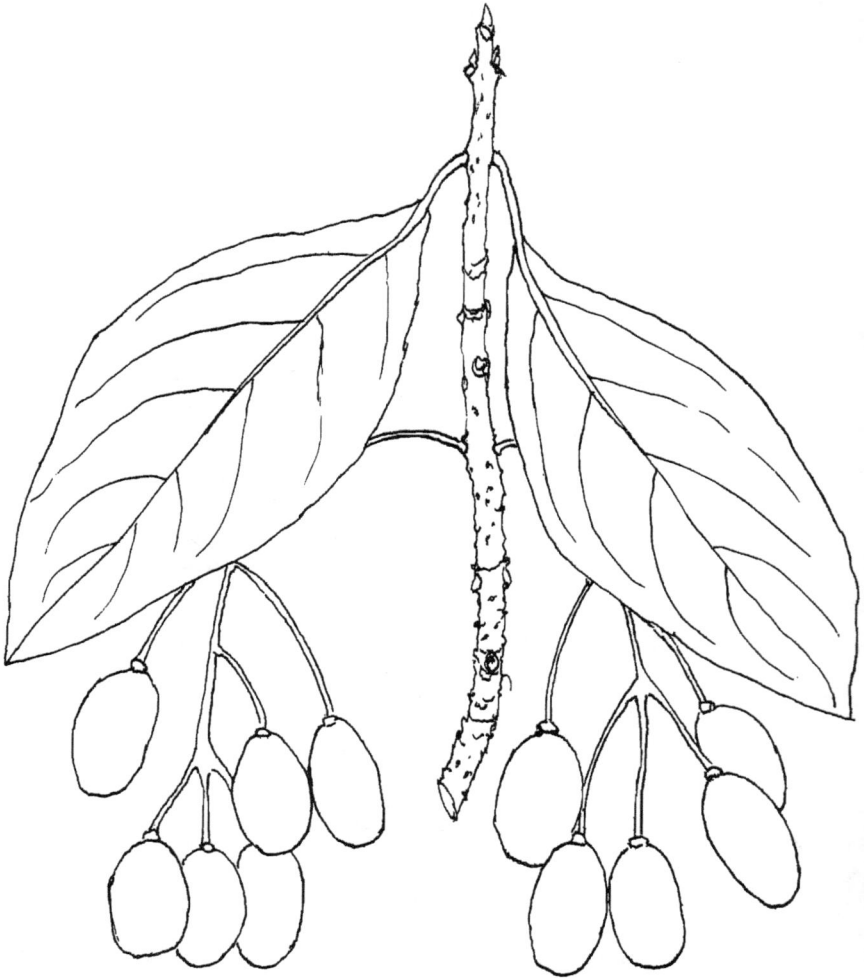

FRINGE TREE.

grown. Because of their beautiful fall color they are
more fully described under The Glory of Autumn. They
are seldom offered by nurseries, but if small ones are

BLACKHAW.

marked before leaves fall, they can be moved from the wild.

The pretty fruits of the various *Viburnums* are eager-ly eaten, and some species last well into winter. Because of their beauty, these have been described in other chapters. *Aralia spinosa* is an odd, prickly shrub, but quite attractive. Usually with one stem, up to twelve feet, it bears a huge panicle of black berries with red stems, and these are favored by a number of birds. It is strange that any creature should care for the dry, sour berries of the Sumacs, but evidently they possess some nutritive value. One bitter winter day, when everything was sheathed in ice, I saw a Sumac bush covered with Bluebirds feasting on this seemingly unpalatable fare. Bluebirds! I was astonished. These big shrubs will grow anywhere, but have to be watched, as they spread by root-runners.

Winter Huckleberry is a standby when weather is unfriendly to the little feathered ones. Many birds feast on the berries, which cling till spring. This is *Vaccinium arboreum*, and may become a low spreading tree. If dug in the wild, very small ones should be selected, for the root is difficult. It grows in dry sandy land, but is adaptable. The red berries of the various Hollies supply food late in winter when most other fruits are gone. The shrub, Yaupon, offers both board and lodging. It is so thickly set with the small evergreen leaves it shuts out wind and rain, and the table is always set with bright red berries. Once I saw a thing that delighted me. Freezing rain had sheathed a Yaupon in ice, but little birds found a way inside. The next morning, cat tracks in the snow went round and round the bush, but they did not find the door! The small occupants were very snug inside.

On large grounds, a Hackberry, *Celtis*, offers a bounteous repast in late winter. The berries are small and dry, but very sweet and appreciated by many birds. In January and February, bird-watchers should get out their binoculars and take a stand under a big Sweetgum. At this time the prickly burs open, spilling out the seeds, and flocks of tiny finches cling upside-down and feast. They constantly give out a little long-drawn "swe-e-et," with an upward inflection. Of course Sweetgums grow very large, so are not for the ordinary garden—a deprivation, for they color gloriously in late fall.

All Finches feed on seeds of grass and weeds—but most of us don't need to plant these! However, the Lespedezas and wild peas can be sown in sunny spots, both for food and beauty.

WINTER HUCKLEBERRY; VACCINIUM ARBOREUM. A FAVORITE "DISH."

SUMMARY, SET THE TABLE FOR THE BIRDS

Wild Cherry, *Prunus serotina*, 4 to 8, except in arid regions. Med. tree.

Mulberry, *Morus rubra*, 5 to 9, except in arid regions. Medium tree.

Common Elder, *Sambucus canadensis*, 3 to 8, east of Colo. Big shrub.

Red Elder, *S. pubens*, all zones n. of N. Georgia, ex. arid regions. Shrub.

Blackberries, Dewberries, Raspberries, etc., some species in every zone.

Pokeberry, *Phytolacca americana*, 4 to 9, e. of Neb. Tall perennial. Acid.

Sassafras albidum (officinale), 4 to 9, e. of Cen. Okla. Medium tree.

Beautyberry, *Callicarpa americana*, 7 to 9, probably 6. Shrub. Dry sites.

Dogwood, *Cornus florida*, 5 to 9, e. of Cen. Okla. Small tree, acid soil.

Blackgum, *Nyssa sylvatica*, 4 to 9, east. Large tree. Slopes. Acid soil.

Blackgum, *N. biflora*, 7 to 9, east. Medium tree, damp ground. Acid.

Aralia spinosa, 5 to 9, east of Cen. Okla. Big shrub. Acid soil.

Sumac, *Rhus copallina*, 4 to 9 east. Big shrub. Well drained sites.

Smooth Sumac, *R. glabra*, 4 to 9 east. Shrub. Rich dry soil.

Staghorn Sumac, *R. hirta (typhina)*, 3 to 7 east. Rich dry soil. Shrub.

Winter Huckleberry, *Vaccinium arboreum*, 6 to 9, e. of
  Cen. Kans. Small tree.
Yaupon, *Ilex vomitorium*, 7 to 9, e. of Cen. Tex. Shrub,
  acid; very adaptable.
Hackberry, *Celtis*, some species in every zone ex. arid
  regions. Trees.
Sweetgum, *Liquidambar styraciflua*, 5 to 9, ex. arid re-
  gions. Big tree.
Blackhaw, *Viburnum rufidulum*, 5 to 8, e. of Colo. Small
  tree. Adaptable.
Shadblows, *Amalanchier*, some species in every zone,
  except arid regions.

WILD AZALEAS, RHODODENDRONS, AND OTHER NATIVE TREES AND FLOWERS ARE MASSED ALONG THE BEAUTIFUL BLUE RIDGE PARKWAY.

ROADSIDES

When I remember roadsides as they used to be, then look at the glaring speedways of today, I ask myself, after all, is *speed* the most important thing in the world? We drove to the country to see the dogwood in spring, the glory of maple and sweetgum in fall. In constructing new highways, engineers have destroyed avenues of ancient Like Oaks, their massive branches locking overhead, when these could have been saved by re-routing the road to one side or the other. Something priceless was wantonly destroyed. Is this "progress"?

The awful gashes made by modern road building look hopeless, but something *can* be done. Where side slopes are steep, the first thing to be considered is erosion control. Sodding with grass is slow and expensive, and the necessary mowing involved very costly. The practical and lasting cover is of native vines and trailing shrubs. A Highway Department in New England wrote me that such plantings had reduced maintenance costs by sixty percent in two years. It is folly to plant highways with Camellias, and cultivated Roses and Azaleas, for these require special care. Our many charming native plants offer the solution, for they are hardy and need little attention.

I have seen steep railroad cuts that were sheets of Yellow Jessamine, *Gelsemium sempervirens*. This beautiful evergreen will trail down banks, and in spring become a mass of fragrant yellow flowers. Wild Roses are effective in holding soil, and are lovely. Prairie Rose, *R. setigera,* is a trailer bearing big clusters of exquisite pink blossoms. The smaller species, such as *R. carolina*

HAWTHORNS (CRATAEGUS, MANY SPECIES)
ARE BEAUTIFUL IN FLOWER AND FRUIT,
AND WILL GROW ALMOST ANYWHERE. IT
WAS ONE OF JENS JENSEN'S FAVORITE
TREES FOR PARK AND ROADSIDE PLANTING.

and *R. humilis,* soon form mats, ideal for holding the soil. The true Cherokee Rose, *R. laevigata,* has shining evergreen leaves, and big white flowers. The long arching canes are graceful and lovély. In the West, two small species, *Rosa foliolosa* and *R. arkansana,* could be effectively used for planting in the alkaline Blacklands.

There are a number of low shrubs that form dense mats, and hold the soil. Beautiful evergreen Yaupon, *Ilex vomitoria,* will grow in most any situation. So will the many species of yellow-flowered St. Johnswort, *Hypericum.* Where the soil is acid, the several species of *Pieris* (*Lyonia*) will flourish. Pretty Burningbush, *Euonymus americanus,* likes similar sites. Wild Gooseberry, *Grossularia campestris,* is a spreader and will soon cover a bank.

In mountainous regions, where soil and rock are cut into tremendous setback terraces, there is no reason why the highest level should not be planted in attractive species of trees. Masses of Dogwood, Redbud, Fringe Tree, and Wild Plum, could be seen and admired by even the speeding motorist. Big shrubs, such as Rhododendrons, Wild Hydrangea, and white and red Buckeye can be charmingly grouped on these big terraces. In the Southwest, "Texas Mountain Laurel," *Sophora secundiflora;* Flowering Willow, *Chilopsis;* and Ceniza, *Leucophylla texanum;* would form a delightful display. By using striking and unusual species, the native charm of each region is thus advertised, and tourists will seek out such drives. People travel far to see the Aspens turn to gold in autumn!

In some places it has been done. Tourists flock by thousands to admire the native Azaleas and Rhodo-

PINES ADD DIGNITY AND BEAUTY TO ANY ROADSIDE.
Photograph by Elemore Morgan.

dendrons along the Blue Ridge Parkway. The Natchez Trace Parkway is becoming more beautiful each year. For years *Magnolia macrophylla,* "the most spectacular flowering tree in the Temperate Zone," has been ruthlessly destroyed. They must be planted back.

In California, slopes along highways can be made beautiful with cascades of blue "Wild Lilacs," the various species of *Ceanothus.* Some are prostrate in habit, and would help control erosion. Bearberry, Creeping Manzanita, is an attractive prostrate shrub which is ideal for covering steep banks in mountainous regions of the West.

All the native trees, shrubs, and vines suitable for roadside planting cannot be given here—the list would be too long. But if highway departments and civic bodies would unite their efforts and use some observation, our roads could become ribbons of beauty, typical of each region. Tourists are drawn from one part of the country to another to see something different, not the monotonous sameness that we have been achieving. The landscaper, Jens Jensen, a famous advocate of native planting, said that by using trees and flowers of each locality, the soul of the country would be revealed.

IN THE SOUTH, STATELY LIVE OAKS ARE PERFECT FOR PARKS AND ROADSIDES.

Photograph by Elemore Morgan.

SUMMARY, ROADSIDES

Yellow Jessamine; *Gelsemium sempervirens.* Evergreen
vine. 7 and 8 east. of Cen. Texas. Sandy, acid soil.

Rosa setigera. Vine. Will grow almost everywhere, except in arid regions.

Cherokee Rose; *Rosa laevigata.* 7 to 9, very adaptable.

Rosa foliolosa. 4 to 8, calcareous soils. Small spreading
shrub.

Rosa arkansana. 4 to 8, calcareous soils. Small spreading
shrub.

Rosa carolina and *R. humilis.* Eastern states. Small
spreading shrub.

Yaupon; *Ilex vomitoria.* 7 to 9 east of Cen. Texas. Evergreen shrub.

St. Johnswort; *Hypericum.* Some species in almost every
zone. Low shrub, yellow flowers.

Pieris nitida (Lyonia). 7 to 9 east. Low spreading evergreen shrub. Acid sandy soil.

Wild Gooseberry; *Grossularia campestris.* 7 to 9. Dry
rocky soil.

Texas Mountain Laurel; *Sophora secundiflora.* Texas.
Rich calcareous soil. Beautiful evergreen shrub,
lavender flowers.

Ceniza; *Leucophylla texanum.* Texas. Rich calcareous
soil. Evergreen shrub.

Flowering Willow; *Chilopsis.* Southwest. Large shrub,
lovely flowers.

Dogwood; *Cornus florida.* 5 to 9, light acid soil, hillsides.
Low tree.

Fringe Tree; *Chionanthus virginica.* 5 to 8 east of Cen.
Okla. Big shrub.

Redbud; *Cercis canadensis*. Almost every zone. Rich soil. Low tree.

Wild Plum; *Prunus*. Some species in every zone, except arid regions.

Rhododendrons, several species. Mountainous regions east, and Northwest Pacific Coast. Light, rich, acid soil. Shrubs.

Wild Hydrangea; *Hydrangea quercifolia*. 7 to 9 east. Shrub, white flowers. Light, rich, acid soil.

White Buckeye; *Aesculus parviflora*. 7 and 8 east. Shrub. Rich soil. High shade.

Red Buckeye; *Aesculus pavia*. 7 to 9, to east Tex. Shrub, red flowers. Sun.

Magnolia macrophylla. 7 to 9 east. Medium tree. Rich soil. Sheltered sites.

Ceanothus prostratus. Northern Pacific Slopes. Creeper. Blue flowers.

Bearberry; *Arctostaphylos uvi-ursi*. 3 to 7, cool regions. Creeping shrub. Acid soil.

GARDEN PICTURES

With their natural grace, native plants lend themselves to the creating of charming effects for each season. Could anything be lovelier than Silverbell (*Halesia*) with a sheet of *Zephyranthes atamasco* beneath? In Florida, Mary Noble has Yuccas rising from a carpet of blue Lupine.

At Arcadia, in North Louisiana, Inez Conger has planned "pictures" for each month. Hers is an up-and-down garden, so is full of delightful surprises. In February, a Shadblow will grace the top of a bank, with those shy beauties, Bloodroot and Hepatica, beneath. In late March the snow of Dogwood lends its blessing to *Phlox divaricata*, Solomon's Seal, Violets and Mayapple, while a steep bank is clothed in the delicate bloom of *Iris cristata*. Wild Crabapple drops its pink petals to mingle with Blue-eyed Grass and Ozark Phlox. The soft white "kitten-tails" of *Itea virginica* are exquisite with colorful Louisiana Iris. In fall, she has Cardinal Flower and blue *Eupatorium* beneath the blazing sprays of *Euonymus americana*.

There is a shade of *Phlox subulata* that matches the brilliant, rather difficult, color of Redbud, *Cercis canadensis*, and the two combined from a stunning picture. The misty white of Fringe Tree is lovely over a carpet of Wild Verbena and the native Phloxes. In early May, the larger *Viburnums* combine beautifully with white *Penstemon digitalis* and Pinkroot (*Spigelia*) .

There are so many desirable combinations of native plants the list is almost endless. On a slope at the edge of my Louisiana Iris garden grows *Zenobia pulverulenta*, with its arching sprays of exquisite snowy bells. And there, too, is a snow-white Mountain Laurel.

In summer we can scatter color lavishly, but even here careful planning is desirable. For example, the wine of Poppy Mallow and orange-red of Butterfly Weed kill each other. The rich color of the Mallow (*Callirhoe papaver*) combines beautifully with the sparkling blue of Dayflower and soft yellow of the low-growing Western Evening Primrose. For blazing color, there are Coralbean (*Erythrina*) and Butterfly Weed, but these need the softening touch of Jersey Tea (*ceanothus*).

In fall, the eye feasts on whole fields of Goldenrod and *Helianthus*. The beauty of autumn color is enhanced by graceful sprays of the many native Asters, in white and lavender.

Elizabeth Lawrence found big pines already growing in her garden, and beneath these, using both cultivated and native plants, she has created some pictures of un- usual beauty. The one that impressed me most was a fine specimen of *Azalea prunifolia*, planted alone where the lovely red of its flowers would not clash with other colors. The brown, grays, and greens of surrounding trees offered the perfect foil for the display.

Also in North Carolina, William Lanier Hunt de- scribes some of his favorite scenes. "A woodsy path leads down a steep hill and comes out suddenly through masses of Fringe Tree gossamer, onto an area snow-white with Atamasco Lilies. A passageway defined by Black Locust trunks slopes down to a mass of the pink Phlox from Louisiana (probably *P. pilosa ozarkana*) and our apple- leaved Carolina Phlox. A path in a woodland garden descends between boulders, at whose feet are carpets of *Shortia*, dainty Oconee Bells."

There are many pictures to be seen at the pond, where everything is reflected in its shining mirror. Even a garden pool repeats and emphasizes the beauty around it. One of the greatest charms of the old gardens around Charleston is the way in which the festooned vines and masses of Azaleas are always duplicated in the dark winding waterways. The late Mary S. Debaillon (Lafayette, Louisiana) also used Cherokee Rose and Yellow Jessamine in her plantings, but placed only the native Azaleas by water. Her entire garden was a series of carefully planned and exquisite pictures.

SUMMARY, GARDEN PICTURES

Silverbell, *Halesia diptera*, 6 to 9, adaptable. Low tree.
Light soil.

Zephyranthes atamasco, 7 to 9 e. of Cen. Tex. Most any
acid soil.

Spanish Dagger, *Yucca aloifolia*, 7 to 9, S'east. Adaptable.

Shadblow, *Amalanchier arborea (canadensis)*, 4 to 9 E.
of Cen. Neb. Low tree.

Bloodroot, *Sanguinaria canadensis*, 5 to 8 e. Shade, good
drainage.

Hepatica americana, 4 to 8 E. Shade. Rich neutral soil.

Dogwood, *Cornus florida*, 5 to 9, E. of Cen. Tex. Small
tree. Light soil.

Solomon's Seal, *Polygonatum biflorum*, 3 to 9 E. of Kans.
Shade. Good soil.

Violets, some sp. in every zone. Most want shade. Various
soils.

Mayapple, *Podophyllum peltatum*, 3 to 9 E. of Neb.
Good soil. Semi-shade.

Iris cristata, 7 and 8 E. Cool rocky slopes. Rich soil.

Wild Crabapples, many sp., all zones except arid regions.
Heavy soil.

Blue-eyed Grass, *Sisyrinchium*, many sp., some in every
zone. Sun. Various soils.

Ozark Phlox, *P. pilosa ozarkana*, Tex., La., and Ark., to
N. C.

Carolina Phlox, *P. carolina*, 7 E. Rich neutral soil.

Kittentails, *Itea virginica*, 7 to 9 E. of Cen. Tex. Shrub.
Low ground.

Louisiana Iris, every zone, with some winter protection
north. Acid soil.

Cardinal Flower, *Lobelia cardinalis,* 3 to 9 E. of Cen. Tex. Moist ground.

Mistflower, *Eupatorium coelestinum,* 5 to 9 E. of Colo. Very adaptable.

Phlox subulata, 3 to 8 E. Very adaptable. Well drained site.

Redbud, *Cercis canadensis,* 3 to 9, E. of Cen. Neb. Rich neutral soil.

Fringe Tree, *Chionanthus virgininica,* 5 to 8 E. of Cen. Okla. Small tree.

Wild Verbena, *V. canadensis,* 5 to 9 E. of Colo. Light soil. Sun.

Verbena tenuisecta, 5 to 9, very adaptable. Sun.

Phlox divaricata, 4 to 9 E. of Neb. Light rich soil. Semi-shade.

Cherokee Rose, *Rosa laevigata,* 7 to 9 E. Likes rich soil, but adaptable.

Yellow Jessamine, *Gelsemium sempervirens,* 7 to 9 E. of Cen. Tex. Vine.

Sou. Blackhaw, *Viburnum rufidulum,* 6 to 9 E. of Cen. Tex. Low tree.

Penstemon digitalis, 4 to 9, probably E. and W., except arid regions.

Pinkroot, *Spigelia marilandica,* 6 to 9 E. of Cen. Okla. Rich soil.

Zenobia pulverulenta, 7 to 9 E. Shrub. Damp ground, acid.

Mountain Laurel, *Kalmia Latifolia,* 5 to 8 & n. part 9. Acid soil. Slopes.

Poppy Mallow, *Callirhoe papaver,* 7 & 8 E. of Cen. Tex. Light soil. Sun.

Butterfly Weed, *Asclepias tuberosa*, 3 to 9 E. and W. Dry soil. Adaptable.

Dayflower, *Commelina angustifolia*, 7 to 9 E. of Cen. Tex. Acid soil. Sun.

Dayflower, *C. crispa*, 5 to 9 E. of Kans. Sandy soil. Sun.

Coralbean, *Erythrina herbacea*, 7 to 9 E. of Cen. Tex. Sandy soil. Sun.

Jersey Tea, *Ceanothus americana*, 4 to 9 E. of Kans. Sandy soil. Sun.

Goldenrods, *Solidago*, many species, some in every zone.

Helianthus angustifolius, 7 to 9. Very adaptable. Acid soil.

Azalea prunifolia, 7 & 8, E. of Tex. Shrub. Rich light soil, acid.

Black Locust, *Robinia pseudoacacia*. Probably in all zones. Medium tree, invasive.

Oconee Bells, *Shortia galacifolia*, 7 & 8, eastern mountains. Shade.

BIBLIOGRAPHY

Cyclopedia of Horticulture, L. H. Bailey.

Trees of North America, C. S. Sargent.

Checklist, Native Trees of the U. S., Department of Agriculture.

Trees of Southeastern States, Coker and Totten.

Flora of Southeastern U. S. (editions II and III), J. K. Small.

New Britton and Brown Flora, Gleason.

Gray's Manual of Botany (8th Ed.), Fernald.

Aristocrats of the Garden, Ernest Wilson.

Bartrams Travels, William Bartram.

Flowers of the South, Greene-Blomquist.

Texas Flowers, Eula Whitehouse.

Florida Wild Flowers, M. F. Baker.

Siftings, Jens Jensen.

Bulletins of the American Rock Garden Society.

Wild Flowers for Your Garden, Helen S. Hull.

Native Plants for the Garden, Brooklyn Botanic Garden.

WHERE TO GET NATIVE PLANTS, BULBS, AND SEEDS

Claude A. Barr, Prairie Gem Ranch, Smithwick, South Dakota. Western plants.

Clyde Robin, P. O. Box 2091, Castro Valley, Cal. Seeds of native trees and flowers.

Gardens of the Blue Ridge, Ashford, North Carolina. Eastern native plants, seeds, and bulbs.

Rex D. Pearce, Moorestown, New Jersey. Native seeds, bulbs, and plants.

Leslie's Wild Flower Nursery, 30 Summer Street, Methuen, Mass. Native plants and seeds, eastern species.

Fruitland Nurseries, Augusta, Georgia. Eastern native shrubs. (A few species.)

The Three Laurels, Marshall, North Carolina. Eastern native shrubs.

S. D. Coleman Nurseries, Fort Gaines, Georgia. Native Azaleas.

Mrs. Ethel Harmon, Saluda, South Carolina. Eastern native plants and bulbs.

Harry Elkins, 916 Westchester, Grosse Point Park 30, Michigan. Eastern native plants.

Tingle Nursery Co., Pittsville, Maryland. Unusual native Azaleas and other beautiful species.

Market Bulletins from Louisiana, Mississippi, Alabama, and Florida.

FOR LOUISIANA IRISES

Mr. Charles Arny, University of Southwestern Louisiana, Lafayette, Louisiana.

University Hills Nursery, 470 Delgado Drive, Baton Rouge, Louisiana.

W. B. McMillan, Abbeville, Louisiana.

Melrose Gardens, Route 1, Box 466, Stockton, Cal.

Mr. J. Patin, Box 51626 O. C. S., Lafayette, La.

INDEX

A

Abies amabilis 96, 104
  " balsamea 104
  " concolor 96
  " fraseri 96, 104
Acer circinatum, 147 ,155
  " floridanum 147, 155
  " glabrum 147, 155
  " negundo 147, 155
  " pennsylvanicum 147, 155
  " rubrum 146, 154, 162
  " rubrum drummondii
    146, 154
Adders Tongue 24
Adiantum pedatum (fern)
  33, 39, 122, 125
Aesculus pavia 71, 91
Agarita 83, 92, 103
Allium coryi 21, 31
  " mutabile 21, 31
Amalanchiers, various 132,
       148, 155, 93
    " canadensis 59, 136,
    148
    " laevis 59
    " sanguinea 59
    " stolonifera 59
Amsonia 46, 51
Anemone caroliniana 26
Aphanostephus skirrobasis 5
Aquilegia canadensis 5, 16, 39

Aralia spinosa 186, 188
Arbor vitae 99
Arbutus menziesii 85
  " arizonica 85, 91
Arctostaphylos uva-ursi 119,
  124, 198
Arisema tryphyllum 18
Aristocrats of the Garden 119
Aronia arbutifolia 130, 135,
    143, 154
  " melanocarpa 143, 154
Arrowhead 129, 134
Asclepias tuberosa 49, 53, 204
Ashe, W. W. 29, 129
Aspen 145, 154
Asters, wild 50, 53, 151
  " wreath 152
Atamasco Lily 200
Athyrium (ferns) 122, 125
Audubon 179
Azaleas, native 33, 89, 127,
  131, 133
Azalea alabamense 78
  " austrina 78, 133, 134
  " calendulaceae 80
  " canescens 78, 133, 134
  " nudiflora 78
  " prunifolia 81, 200, 204
  " serrulata 80
  " viscosa 78

B

Bailey's Encyclopedia 96, 118
Baptisias 46
Barberries 140, 153
Barr, Claude 7, 11, 22, 23, 24,
  26, 170
Bartram's Travels 76
Bearberry 119, 124, 195, 198
Beautyberry 157, 182, 188
Beech 148, 155

Beggartick, Creeping 119, 124
Berberis trifoliata 83, 92, 103
Berchemia scandens 108, 114
Betula papyrifera 157, 162
Bignonia capreolata 108, 114
  " radicans 108, 114
Birch, White 152, 162
Bittersweet 109, 114
Blackberry 182

Blackgum 145, 154, 183, 188
Blackhaw 185
Black Lands 22
Bleeding Heart 5, 16
Blomquist 20
Bloodroot 8, 18, 36, 41, 199, 202
Bluebells, Virginia 18
Blueberries 150
Bluebonnets, Texas 44, 51
Blue-eyed Grass 27, 199, 202
Bog Torches 127
Box Elder 147, 155
Bradburya virginiana 113, 115, 120

Bryant, William Cullen (To a Fringed Gentian) 151
Buckeyes, several, 193, 198
Buckeye, Red 71, 91
   "   White 72, 148, 152, 155
   "   , Yellow 72
Buffalo Berry 143
Burning Bush 143
Buttercups 21, 27
Butterfly Lilies 22
   "   Tulips 22
   "   Weed 49, 53, 200, 204

C

Calacanthus florida 74, 91, 148, 155
   "   occidentalis 74
Callicarpa 137, 182, 188
Callirhoe papaver 47, 52, 200, 203
   "   involucrata 47, 52
Calochortus gunnisoni 22, 31
   "   nuttallii 22, 31
   "   vesta 22, 31
Camassia esculenta 25, 31
   "   hyacinthina 25, 32
Campanula rotundiflora 35, 41
Cardinal Flower 33, 39, 171, 177
Carruth, M. S. 12, 21
Carya alba 145, 154, 157, 162
Cassiope 7, 18
Castilleja coccinea 171, 174
Cattails 129
Ceanothus americanus 49, 52, 87, 200, 204
   "   azureus 81, 118, 124
   "   fendleri 118, 124
   "   hirsutus 87

Ceanothus prostratus 118, 124
   "   spinosus 87
   "   thrysflorus 87
Cedar, Red 198
Celastrus scandens 109, 114
Celestials 16, 24, 84, 171, 193
Celtis, various 189
Ceniza 84, 193
Centauria americana 168, 174
Cercis canadensis 198, 199, 203
Charleston, old gardens 200
Cheilanthes (fern) 12, 18
Cherry, Wild 182, 188
Chilopsis linearis 84, 92, 193
Chionanthus virginica 62
Chokeberry, Red 130, 135
Cimicifuga racemosa 35, 41
Cladrastis lutea 67, 89
Claytonia 27, 32
Clematis coccinea 112, 115
   "   crispa 112, 115
   "   texana 112, 115
   "   virginiana 112, 115
Clethra 129
Cliftonia monophylla 67, 91, 102

Clint, Mrs. Morris 21
Cocculus carolinianum 112, 114
Columbines 16, 33
Commelina angustifolia 49, 52, 204
    "   crispa 49, 52
Coneflower, Pale 45, 51
Conger, Inez (Mrs. W. E.) 15, 120, 180, 199
Cooperia pedunculata 21, 31
Cornel, Dwarf 123, 125
Cornus asperifolia 138
    "   canadensis 122, 125
    "   florida 6, 38, 183, 188
    "   "   rubra 6
    "   nuttallii 61, 86

Cornus racemosa 138
    "   stolonifera 138
Crabapples, various 63, 92, 199
Crataegus (various) 93, 140
    "   aestivalis 63
    "   apiifolia 141
Crataegus brachycantha 63, 142, 159
    "   cordata 141
    "   crus-galli 141
    "   marshallii 141
    "   punctata 142
    "   spathulata 141
Crinum americanum 27, 32
Crossvine 103, 104
Cullowhee 20
Cyrilla racemiflora 66, 91

D

Dayflower 49, 52, 200, 204
Debaillon, Mary Swords 79, 201
Delphinium carolinianum 46, 51
Dewberry 182
Dicentra canadensis 5, 16, 37, 43
    "   cuccularia 5, 16, 37, 43

Dichondra 117, 124
Dodecatheon 41, 46, 51
Dogtooth Violet 23
Dogwood, various 61, 90, 162, 183, 188, 193
    "   , osier 159
    "   , white-fruited 183
Dormon, Ruth 6, 24, 171
Dutchman's Breeches 5, 16, 37, 43

E

Echinaceae pallida 45, 51, 167, 173
    "   purpurea 46, 167
Elderberry 86, 94
Elder, Blueberry 74
    "   , common 74, 137; 154
    "   , Pacific Red 74
    "   , Red 74, 137, 153
Elders, various 182

Elm, White 157, 162
    " , Cork 157, 162
    " , Winged 157, 162
Epstein, Harold 6, 11
Eryngium leavenworthii 46, 51, 166, 173
Erythrina herbacea 48, 52, 200, 204

Erythronium americanum 18,
    23, 31
  "   albidum 23, 31
  "   californicum 23, 31
  "   giganteum 23, 31
  "   johnsonii 23, 31
  "   mesochorium 23, 31
  "   oregonum 11, 18
  "   revolutum 11, 18

Euonymus americana 143,
    154, 193, 199
Eupatorium coelestinum 50,
    53, 199, 203
Eustoma russellianum 46, 51,
    165, 173
Eustylis purpurea 25, 31, 170,
    173
Evans, Jo (Mrs. U. B.) 180
Evening Primroses 44, 170

F

Fagus grandifolia 148, 155
Fairy Lanterns 22
Fawn Lily 24
Fern, Christmas 122, 125, 35,
    39
  "   , Lady 122
  "   , Maidenhair 122, 125
  "   , Shield 122
Fernow, B. E. 39, 96
Figworts 171
Fir, Balsam 96, 104
  " , Lovely 96, 104

Fir, Silver 96, 104
  " , White 96
Fischer, David 30
Flora of Southeastern States,
    Small 85
Fothergilla major, 67
  "   monticola 67
Fothergillas 91
Franklinia alatamaha 76
Fremontia californica 86
French Mulberry 137
Fringe Tree 62, 193, 200, 203

G

Gaillardias 44
Galax aphylla 5, 8, 16, 36, 41
Gaultheria procumbens 119,
    124
Gayfeather 168
Gelsemium sempervirons 107,
    111, 114, 124, 191
Gentian, Closed 37, 43, 131,
        133, 135, 151
  "   , Fringed 151, 156
Gentiana andrewsii 43, 152,
        155
  "   saponaria 43, 151,
    155, 156

Gerardia, Purple 171, 174
  "   , Yellow 171
Gilia, Blue 47
  "   , rubra 52, 165, 173
  "   , Scarlet 47, 52, 165, 173
Ginger, Wild 16, 120, 125
Gladney, Mrs. Frank 78
Goldenrods, various 50, 53,
        200, 204
  "   , Wreath 37, 43
Gooseberry, Wild 193
Gordonia lasianthus 76
Grapes, various 109, 114
Grossularia campestris 193

H

Habenaria ciliaris 128, 134
Habranthus texana 21, 31
Hackberry, various 186, 189
Halesia diptera 63, 91
    ”   carolina 63, 91
Harebells, Hairbells 35, 41
Harmon, Mrs. Ethel 20
Hartmannia 170
Haw, Parsley 62
    ” , spatulate-leaved 62
Hawthorns 62, 93, 140, 153
Heath Family 151
Helianthus angustifolius 52,
    132, 136, 168, 173, 200, 204
Hemlock, Canada 98
    ”   , carolina 98
Henry, Mrs. Cammie 84, 171
    ”   , Mary G. 6, 12

Hepatica 8, 18, 36, 41, 199,
    202
Herbertia caerulea 24, 31
Hibiscus, various 49, 53
    ”   moscheutos 50, 53
Hickory, White 145, 149, 154,
    157
Hoak, Charlotte 23
Hollies, various 186
Holly, American 100, 142
    ” , Dahoon 100
Huckleberries, various 69, 182
Huckleberry, Winter 150, 155,
    186, 189
Hunt, William Lanier 200
Hymenocallis Eulae 28
    ”   rotatum 28
Hypericums, various 193

I

Ilex ambigua (or caroliniana)
    143
    ·· cassine 100
    ·· longipes
    ·· montana 143, 153
    ·· verticillata 142, 153
    ·· vomitoria 100, 193
Ilexes, deciduous 142
Ilicium floridanum 57, 91, 102
Indian Paintbrush 44, 171,
    174
Ipomoea macrorhiza 112, 115
    ··   pandurata 112, 115,
    120, 124
Iris bracteata 177, 181
    ·· (Louisiana), Bayou Ver-
    milion 178
    ” brevicaulis 175, 178

Iris cristata 175, 181, 199, 202
    ” douglasiana 177, 181
    ” fulva 178, 181
    ” giganticaerulea 178
    ” (Louisiana), Kramer
    Yellow 178
    ·· (Louisiana), Haile Selas-
    sie 178
    ·· (Louisiana), Jeune Fille
    178
    ·· missouriensis 177, 181
    ·· prismatica 177, 181
    ·· tenax 177, 181
    ·· tripetala 128, 133, 134
    ·· versicolor 177, 181
    ” virginica 177, 181
Itea virginica 129, 134, 199,
    202

J

Jack-in-the-pulpit 8, 18, 33, 39
Jensen, Jens 195

Jersey Tea 49, 52, 200, 204
Juniperus virginiana 64, 98

K

Kalmia latifolia 81, 89, 102
Kell, Willie Mae 21, 22, 84
Kitten-tails 129, 199, 202

Klaber, Doretta 15
Kruckeberg, Dr. 9

L

Lambdin, Mary (Mrs. S. H.) 27
Lambert, John 11
Larkspur, Wild 44, 46
Lawrence, Elizabeth 8, 12, 21, 22, 200, 245
Lazy Daisy 44, 57
Leiophyllum buxifolium 118, 124
Lespedeza 187
Leucophylla texanum 24, 92, 193
Leucothoe axillaris 102
      " catesbaei 35, 43, 103
      " recurva 71
Liatris, various 46, 50, 168
Lilacs, Wild 86
Lilium canadense 29, 32
      " carolinianum 29, 32
      " catesbaei 29, 32
      " grayii 29, 32
      " humboldtii 30, 32

Lilium michauxii 29, 32, 35, 41
      " pardalinum 30, 32
      " philadelphicum 29, 32
      " superbum 28, 32
      " washingtonianum 30, 32
Lily, Carolina 29, 35, 41
Liquidambar styriciflua 145, 154, 159, 162
Liriodendron tulipifera 57, 90, 148, 155, 159, 162
Lobelias 172
      " cardinalis 33, 39, 171, 174
Locust, Black 200, 204
Lonicera sempervirens 108, 114
Lupinus diffusus 167, 173
      " perennis 167, 173
      " texensis 51, 167, 173
Lycopodium 122, 125
Lyonia nitida 43, 102

M

Madronas 85
Magnolia acuminata 57, 89
      " cordata 57
      " fraseri 56, 89
      " grandiflora 55, 99, 100
      " macrophylla 56, 89, 165, 195
      " pyramidata 29, 57, 89
      " virginiana (glauca) 55, 89

Mahonia aquifolia 87
      " pinnata 87
      " repens 87, 119, 124
Maidenhair fern 33, 39
Mallow, Poppy 200, 203
Malus angustifolia 63
      " coronaria 63
Mamou 47, 49, 52
Manzanita, Creeping 195
Maple, mountain 147, 155
      " , Red 146, 154, 157, 162
      " , Silver 146, 154

Maple, Sugar 146, 154
" , striped 47, 135
" , vine 147
Maples, various 46, 149, 155
Mayapple 33, 39, 199, 202
Maypop 113, 115
McMillan, W. B. 179
Meadow-sweet 72
Meibomia michauxii 119, 124
Melampodium 11, 18
Mertensia virginica 5, 18, 33, 57
Mesquite 84, 91
Midden Morning Glory 113
Millais, J. G. 56
Mistflower 203

Mitchella repens 35, 41, 131, 135
Monarda didyma 33, 46, 49
" fistulosa 51
More Aristocrats of the Garden 139
Morus rubra 188
Mountain Ash 140, 153
Mountain Laurel 3, 12, 39, 81, 127, 134, 200, 203
Mountain mariposa 22
Mulberry 182, 188
Muir, John 96
Myrica certifica 101
" pennsylvanica 101

N

Nelumbo lutea 131
Nemastylis geminiflora 16, 24, 31
Nichols, Mrs. May 21, 169

Nympheaes, several 131
Nyssa sylvatica 145, 183, 188
" biflora 183, 188

O

Oak, Laurel 101
" , Live 100, 101
" , Scarlet 152, 155
" , Water 101, 157, 162
" , White 152, 155
" , Willow 101
Oconee Bells 16
Oenothera biennis 17
" speciosa 46, 51, 174
" rhombipetala 170, 174

Olive, Wild Sweet 101
Onion, Wild 21
Orchid, Yellow Fringed 128, 134
Orontium aquaticum 127, 134
Osmanthus americanus 101
Osmundas (ferns) 122, 125
Oswego Tea 33
Oxalis violaceae 26, 32
Oxydendron arboreum 69, 89, 144, 154

P

Pachysandra procumbens 122, 125
Parcher, Emily 149
Partridgeberry 41
Partridge Pea (pink) 113, 115, 119

Passiflora incarnata 113, 115
" lutea 113, 115
Passion Flower 113, 115
" " , Dwarf 113, 115
Pearce, F. O. 7

Penstemon digitalis 51, 169, 173, 199
   ,,   murrayanus 169, 173
   ,,   western 44, 51, 169
   ,,   white 49, 169, 173, 199
Phlox allyssifolia 7, 121, 125
  ,,   andicola 7, 16
  ,,   bifida 7
  ,,   carolina 200, 202
  ,,   divaricata 16, 33, 39
  ,,   douglasi 7, 16
  ,,   hoodii 7
  ,,   longifolia 7
  ,,   pilosa 6
  ,,   ,,   ozarkana 6, 200
  ,,   stolonifera 16, 121, 125
  ,,   ,,   , var. Blue Ridge 6
  ,,   subulata 16, 121, 125
Photinia arbutifolia 103, 144
Phyllodoce 7, 18
Picea canadensis 98, 104
  ,,   mariana 97, 104
  ,,   pungens 98, 104
Pickerel Weed 129, 134
Pieris lucida (or nitida) 35, 43, 127, 134
Pinckneya pubens 129, 132, 134
Pine, Loblolly 104
  ,,   , Longleaf 95, 104, 132
  ,,   ' Pinon 96
  ,,   , Silver 104

Pine, Slash 104
  ,,   , Spruce 95
  ,,   , White 96
Pinewoods Lily 25
Pinkroot 33, 39, 199, 203
Pinus caribaea 104
  ,,   edulis 96, 104
  ,,   glabra 95, 104
  ,,   monticola 96
  ,,   strobus 96, 104
  ,,   taeda 95, 104
Plums, Wild 59, 93, 193
Podophyllum peltatum 39, 202
Pokeberry 182
Polystichum acrostichoides (fern) 35, 39, 122
  ,,   braunei 35, 41 (fern)
  ,,   lonchitis (fern) 35, 41
Pomette Blue 142, 153
Pontederia cordata 129, 134
Poppy, Castilleja 49, 52
  ,,   , Prickly 49, 52
Populus tremuloides 145, 154
Potato, Wild 112, 115, 120, 124
Prosopis 91
Prunus americana 59
  ,,   mexicana 59
  ,,   serotina 188
  ,,   umbellata 59, 159, 163

Q

Quercus alba 155, 157, 162
  ,,   coccinea 152, 155
  ,,   laurifolia 100

Quercus nigra 157, 162
  ,,   virginiana 100

R

Rain-lilies 21
Ranunculus apricus 27, 32

Ranunculus macranthus 27, 32

Rattan, 108, 114
Redbud 93, 198
Redroot 49
Rheder, Alfred 118
Rhexias, various 128, 134
Rhododendron carolinianum
                   83
       "   catawbiense
                   83
       "   maxima 82
       "   minus 83
Rhus copallina 144, 154
  "   glabra 144, 154
  "   hirta 144, 154
  "   vernix 144
Robinia pseudoacacia 204
Rock Daisy 11, 18
Rock Garden Society, American 15

Rosa arkansana 11, 12, 18,
    118, 124, 193
  "   bracteata 111, 114
  "   foliolosa 11, 18, 118, 124,
      193
  "   humilis 193
  "   laevigata 111, 114, 138,
      193, 201, 203
  "   setigera 111, 114, 191
Rose, Cherokee 111, 114, 201,
    203
  " , Prairie 111, 114, 191
Rudbeckia hirta 44, 52, 167,
    178
  "   maxima 168
  "   triloba 168, 173
Ruellia ciliosa 7

S

Sabbatia angularis, 44, 47, 52
Salvia azureus 47, 52
  "   coccinea 47, 52
  "   greggii 85, 92
Sambucus callicarpa 74, 86
  "   canadensis 74, 137,
      153, 188
  "   glauca 74, 86
  "   pubens 131, 153,
  182
Sand Myrtle 118, 124
Sanguinaria canadensis 18, 41,
  52, 202
Sassafras officinale 182, 188
Saururus cernuus 129, 134
Shadblows, various 93, 132,
  149, 155
Shady Gardens (Parcher) 149
Shanks, Mrs. Oscar 166, 173
Shepherdia argentia 143, 154
Shieldfern 35, 41
Shootingstars 35, 41, 46, 51,
  171

Shortia 5, 8, 36, 43, 200, 204
Silene caroliniana 8, 16
  "   stellata 49, 52
  "   subciliata 170
  "   wherryii 8, 16
Silverbell 142, 199
Sisyrinchium 202
Smilax, Southern 111, 114
  "   Red-berried 111, 114
  "   lancifolia 111, 114
  "   lanciolata 111, 114
  "   walterii 111, 114
Snowbell 63, 91
Snowberry 140, 153
Sloe 159
Solidago, various 53, 200, 204
Solomon's Seal 36, 41, 199,
  202
Sophora affinis 84, 92
  "   secundiflora 83, 92,
  103, 193
Sorbus americana 120, 153
Sourwood 69, 89, 144, 154

Sphagnum Moss 127
Spiderlily 32
Spiderwort 46, 51
Spigelia marilandica 33, 39,
    199, 203
Spiraea alba 72
    "   densiflora 72
    "   menziesii 72
    "   tomentosa 72
Spleenworts (ferns) 12, 19
Spring Beauty 21, 27, 31
Spruce, Colorado Blue   96,
        104
    "   , Black 97, 104
    "   , White 104
Squirrel Corn 5, 16, 37, 43
Star Anise 91, 95, 157, 202
Steeplebush 72, 94

Stewartia malocodendron 78
Steyermark, Dr. Julian 26
Storm, Mrs. A. F. 78
Strophostyles umbellata 119,
    124
Stylrax grandifolia 63, 91
Sumac, Fragrant 119, 124
    "   , Poison 144
    "   , Staghorn 144, 154
Swamp Candles 127, 139
Sweetgum 145, 149, 154, 159,
    197
Sweet Shrub 74, 91, 148, 156
Sycamore 157
Symphocarpos albus (or race-
            mosa) 140, 153
    "   , occidentalis
    140

Taylor, Mrs. Fred 30
Taxus canadensis 98
Texas Bluebell 46, 51, 65, 173
    " Mountain Laurel 83
    "   Plume 165, 173
    "   Bluebonnets 167, 173
Thuga occidentalis 99
Titi 67, 91, 102
Toyon 103, 144
Tradescantia bracteata 46, 51
Trichel, Mrs. Lillian 24, 85
Trillium erectum 8, 18

Trillium grandiflorum 8, 18
    "   luteum 8, 18
    "   sessile 18
    "   stylosum 8, 18
    "   undulatum 18
Trout Lily 24
Trumpetvine 104, 108
Tsuga canadensis 98
    "   caroliniana 98
Turkeyberry 117, 124, 135
Twinberry 117
Typha 129

Ulmus alata 157, 162

Ulmus americana 157, 162

Vaccinium arboreum 69, 150,
        152, 186, 189
    "   elliotti 69, 149,
        155

Vaccinium frondosum 69
    "   pallidum 69
    "   vitis-idaea 37

Verbena canadensis 7
   "   tenuisecta 8, 18, 122, 125
   "   venosa 122
Viburnum acerifolium 64, 139, 152
   "   alnifolium 66, 139
   "   americanum 66, 139
   "   cassinoides 65, 131, 135, 153
   "   dentatum 65
   "   nudum 65, 129, 135, 153

Viburnum obovatum 66
   "   prunifolium 65
   "   rufidulum 65, 139, 153, 189
   "   scabrellum 65, 139
Vinca minor 117, 124
Viola papilionaceae 120
   "   priceana 120
   "   striata 120
Violets, various 3, 16, 36
Violets, White 131
Virginia Creeper 109, 114
Vitis, various 114

W

Waterlilies 131
Wax Myrtle 101
Wherry, Dr. Edgar T. 7
Whitehouse, Eula 25, 27
Wild Easter Lily 20
Wild Ginger 5, 35, 41
Wild Lilacs 117, 124
Willow, Flowering 24, 92

Wilson, Ernest 82, 139, 140
Winecups, 47
Winterberry 142, 153
   "   , Mountain 143
Wintergreen 119, 124
Wistaria frutescens 107
Witch Hazel 76, 94, 149, 155
Woodsia (fern) 12, 18

Y

Yaupon 100, 186, 189, 193
Yellow Jessamine 107, 114, 117, 124, 191, 203

Yellow-wood 67
Yew, Canada 98
Yucca treculeana 85

Z

Zenobia pulverulenta 71, 89, 199, 203

Zephyranthes, atamasco 20, 31, 199, 202
Zinnia grandiflora 11, 18

www.ingramcontent.com/pod-product-compliance
Lightning Source LLC
Chambersburg PA
CBHW060336100426
42812CB00003B/1008